Dale Ralph Davis is amo
Testament alive today. F
infectious. A pastor at he.
by an absolute loyalty to the text, a belief that the Bible
was written for today as much as yesterday, and a desire to
encourage his readers to fall in love with Scripture and to trust
it. These expositions of Psalms 13–24 tantalizingly suggest
there may be further volumes given the enormous success of
the first set (Ps. 1–12). What a treasure that would be! In the
meantime, these expositions are pure gold.

Derek W. H. Thomas
Senior Minister, First Presbyterian Church
Columbia, South Carolina

I shall never forget the first time one of the commentaries of
Dale Ralph Davis was my Bible reading companion.

He made the Scripture I was reading come alive with
his inimitable combination of exegetical and linguistic skills
finding a conduit of expression that was homileticly clear,
fresh, gripping, and often illuminated with historical inci-
dents, earthy anecdotes and chastened humor. I found myself
continually leaving my study (located in my home) to find
my wife somewhere in the house and share with her a few
sentences or a paragraph from that particular commentary
which was too rich and helpful to keep to myself.

This latest book by Dr. Davis opens up Psalm 13–24 with
the same unique characteristics that have endeared the man
and his Old Testament commentaries to so many of us. Thank
you Dr. Davis, for 'yielding to the temptation' to continue
what you began with Psalm 1–12.

Albert N. Martin
Former pastor of Trinity Baptist Church
Montville, New Jersey

Always fresh, always insightful. Dale Ralph Davis shows you what's there and leaves you wondering why you didn't see it before!

Colin Smith
Senior Pastor, The Orchard Evangelical Free Church
President of *Unlocking the Bible*
Arlington, Illinois

Dale Ralph Davis has provided another faithful, lively and refreshing set of expositions. All Christians will benefit from this book and I hope it is read widely.

Sam Allberry
Associate Minister, St Mary's Church
Author of *Connected: Living in the Light of the Trinity*, and *Is God Anti-Gay?*
Maidenhead, England

Sharp, personal and funny illustrations, a vital, earnest and readable style, deep, nourishing, practical application built on a foundation of passionately thorough biblical, theological and linguistic scholarship. When I try to describe to my friends what I love about the writings of Dale Ralph Davis, out comes this curious cocktail. When I add, 'And I guarantee you'll laugh out loud!' my flummoxed friends are left wondering, 'What sort of serious bible commentary *is* this?!?' My answer is, 'The very best sort!' Be you pastor, ploughman, plumber, professor – as Dale Ralph Davis explains, expounds, applies and reflects upon Psalm 13–24, your own slog along the path of righteousness stands to be challenged, expanded, enriched and encouraged. 126 Psalms to go, Ralph!

Colin Buchanan
Christian Children's Recording Artist and author
Sydney, Australia

Those of us who have long valued Ralph Davis' ministry of the Word both written and spoken will welcome more of the same in this exposition of Psalms 13–24. His engaging style and his gift for apt (often hilarious) illustration are here again, in full measure, and behind them you are aware of that rare combination, awesome scholarship (the man has read and evaluated *everything*!) together with a passion for hearing and passing on in a thoroughly down-to-earth style what God is saying to His church today.

Michael Wilcock
Author, Formerly director of pastoral studies at Trinity College
Eastbourne, England

True worship is, as Dale Ralph Davis puts it in this brilliantly helpful book on Psalms 13–24, 'from the top down'. So the same has to be true of our devotional reading of God's word. Our true comfort, our deep encouragement to persevere, our solid growth in trust amidst the mayhem of life all start with God as he has spoken in his word. It's this capacity to draw fresh devotional truths from the deep well of the biblical text that is the author's great gift. Here is a fellow-traveller who is realistic and properly grounded on the same planet that the rest of us occupy, refreshing us along God's way with God's revealed and written truth. So the author's profound understanding of what the text of the Psalms means leads to profound help with what the Psalms really do mean *for you*. Dale Ralph Davis has these two things the right way round. This book is an absolute gem!

Dominic Smart
Author and conference speaker

SLOGGING ALONG
IN THE
PATHS
OF
RIGHTEOUSNESS

Psalms 13–24

Dale Ralph Davis

Copyright © Dale Ralph Davis

paperback ISBN 978-1-78191-304-8
epub ISBN 978-1-78191-332-1
Mobi ISBN 978-1-78191-333-8

10 9 8 7 6 5 4 3 2 1

Printed in 2014, reprinted in 2016
by
Christian Focus Publications Ltd.,
Geanies House, Fearn, Ross-shire,
IV20 1TW, Scotland, Great Britain
www.christianfocus.com

Cover design by
Daniel Van Straaten

Printed by Bell & Bain, Glasgow

MIX
Paper from
responsible sources
FSC® C007785

CONTENTS

PREFACE

I was not going to write up another set of expositions on Psalms after *The Way of the Righteous in the Muck of Life* on Psalms 1–12. But the next dozen psalms were just sitting there and they tempted me. When the Bible tempts you, you should always yield. So I did.

Once again, I have tried to keep the style informal and conversational and footnote-less. I have frequently included shortened notes to sources in brackets—just enough in case readers want to track down a reference.

The title of this collection tries to bring together twin realities: that the Lord's servant is called to live faithfully (being led and walking in 'the paths of righteousness') and that much of it is slow going (slogging along), simply wading through a bunch of trouble (note, for example, Psalms 13, 17, 22).

I would like to offer this little book as a tribute to the memory of my mother-in-law, Frances Herron, whom I esteem increasingly as the years pass. Heartache did not pass her by. Her first husband died on the farm when he was kicked by a mule; leukemia apparently took her three-year-old boy; later her oldest son, eighteen, was electrocuted in a farm-related incident. Who can tell how staggering these blows must have been? And I can't pinpoint where in this mix that Mom came to Christ. There was surely a hand that held her up. Here was a woman who had to walk through the valley of the shadow of death repeatedly and yet, for all that, never stopped following Christ in the paths of righteousness. I can only be deeply grateful. She is evidence that grace is tougher than I have ever imagined.

Psalm 13

For the music leader. A psalm of David.

(1) How much longer, Yahweh, will you go on forgetting me?
     Forever?
     How much longer will you go on hiding your face from me?

(2) How much longer must I lay plans within me
     —agony in my heart by day?
     How much longer will my enemy be lifted up over me?

(3) Look! Answer me, Yahweh, my God!
     Give light to my eyes, lest I sleep in death;

(4) lest my enemy should say, 'I have trounced him!';
     lest my adversaries rejoice because I stagger.

(5) But I, I have trusted in your unfailing love;
     let my heart rejoice in your salvation!

(6) I will sing to Yahweh,
     for he has cared so completely for me.

1

Faith: From Anguish to Assurance

My older brothers grew up in a small western Pennsylvania town where their father was the United Presbyterian pastor. (He was my father too, but that was a good bit later—I was an apparent 'accident'.) They all went to what was essentially a one-room schoolhouse with at least eight grades all in the main room. Years later, as a young fellow, I loved the times when several of my brothers would be together and start reminiscing of school days in Sheakleyville. They told of items that were put into the school's pot-bellied stove in wintertime. A bit noisy but nothing fatal. They would tell how older kids persuaded and goaded their youngest brother (at the time) to sass the teacher and how he got punished for it. They would rehearse one escapade after another; it was grand entertainment. Once, when I was a very young teenager—after our family had long moved away from the original scene of these crimes—and after one of these

'Remember when…' sessions by my brothers, my mother strictly charged me that I was to disclose none of these stories to anyone! What was her problem? Her concern was that, though we were not 'much,' our family should be scrupulous about its reputation and the last thing we needed was a bunch of tarnishing tales from the past making the rounds. It was damage control. There were certain things that were not to get out. Now what if the editors of the Psalms had come upon Psalm 13 and said, 'Whoa! This implies bleak despair may be part of believing experience. Do you think we ought to let that get out?'

That's why this heading to Psalm 13 never looked so good! It tells us that this psalm was authorized for use in Israel's worship. Some do seem to have problems with it. Charles Spurgeon at least chides David for the way he speaks in the opening verses, but even Spurgeon was wrong sometimes. And the psalm even made the cut in my own denomination's hymnal: it's right there, No. 641— *How long wilt thou forget me, O Lord, thou God of grace?* How glad we should be to have these worn and tear-stained pages as a stated part of this prayer book of the Bible; how happy we should be that these desperate pleas with raw nerves hanging all over them escaped the censor's knife!

Let's wade into this prayer behind David, who may well teach us to pray and show us something of the path from anguish to assurance.

Notice that right at the first David pulls us into the **weariness faith knows (vv. 1–2)**. He is in triple trouble—well, anguish is seldom simple. His trouble is with God ('How much longer, Yahweh, will you go on forgetting me…will you go on hiding your face from me?',

v. 1); with self ('How much longer must I lay plans within me—agony in my heart by day?', v. 2a); and with enemies ('How much longer will my enemy be lifted up over me?', v. 2b). I suppose you could dub these the theological, psychological, and sociological aspects of David's distress respectively, but I doubt that clinical analysis would help him much. Absence of God, anxiety of soul, supremacy of the enemy—that is the bundle of trouble he has. Without doubt, the first of those is the most galling and appalling of all.

Philip Yancey, in his book on prayer, tells of Karl, an Air Force officer who suffered head, back, and spinal injuries in a cycling accident. As a result, he was paralyzed from the chest down and began to endure life from a wheelchair, with no bladder or bowel control, facing muscle spasms and infections, having steel rods implanted in his spinal column. But that, Karl said, was not the worst. The most severe suffering was that God's presence was withdrawn. Karl said he still went on praying and believing but there was no sense of God's presence. Being decimated is one thing; being abandoned is far worse.

That may be the worst part of David's trouble but not all of it. He lays plans, with agony in his heart (v. 2a); that is, he conjures up possible options or 'solutions' to his troubles; he becomes consumed with proposed scenarios of plans A, B, C, etc., all of which are dead-end streets. And then to top it all off, there's the mockery and gloating of his enemy (v. 2b).

But it's worse than that. Four times David asks, 'How much longer...?' It's also a problem of timing and he's wrestling with Yahweh's 'delays.' It's one matter to wade through crud and darkness and anxiety and mockery, but when you never seem to come out on the other end, when you seem to be marooned in the thick of the mess and hanging on by your fingernails and days pass and nothing changes and God doesn't meet your last conceivable deadline before you cave in—what then? 'How much longer?' The danger is not that we will blow out but wear out. Besides all else, we have troubles with God's timing—we go on in our troubles far longer than we think the mercy of God would allow. Tell me, then, as you read these two verses of Psalm 13—does the Bible understand us or what?

But then notice, secondly, **the instinct faith follows (v. 3a)**. Did you really hear verses 1-2? And now do you really see verse 3a? Do you sense a logical disconnect? Let's trace the psalm so far, as if it has been you who has been praying. You pray and pray and God does not pay attention; He hides His face, you say; you plead and cry and there is no relief. So what do you do? You go right on praying, of course! To whom? To the God who has not heard. Is there any other? This is lousy logic but excellent faith. You are convinced that Yahweh is forgetting you and hiding His face from you in your misery; and the next thing you do is to cry, 'Look! Answer me, Yahweh my God!' In one way, it seems senseless. You bemoan a God who is not paying attention to you and then in the next breath you nevertheless plead for Him to pay attention. It may not seem rational but it's revealing. Strictly speaking, there may be times when faith does not have its reasons, but it still has its reactions. I call this the instinct of faith. Even when Yahweh seems to turn a deaf ear to us, a believer will simply keep coming back to Him. It's almost a spiritual knee-jerk reaction. And sometimes our instincts are very revealing and comforting.

I like that story Charles Spurgeon told about the woman in his first congregation at Waterbeach. He called her Mrs. Much-afraid. She was always doubting and fearful over her spiritual condition, though she had been a believer for fifty years and showed all the fruit of a genuine faith. She was faithful in worship, helpful to neighbors, willing to speak to the unconverted. One day they were talking, and she declared she had no hope, no faith, and feared she was a hypocrite. So Spurgeon told her to quit coming to the chapel, because 'we don't want hypocrites there.' He asked her why she came. She replied, 'I come because I can't stop away. I love the people of God; I love the house of God; and I love to worship God.' Spurgeon assured her that she was an odd sort of hypocrite. As the conversation moved on, he asked if she had no hope at all. 'No,' she said. So Spurgeon pulled out his wallet, and said: 'Now, I have got five pounds here, it is all the money I have, but I will give you that five pounds for your hope if you will sell it.' She looked at him, evidently puzzled, but then exclaimed, 'Why! I would not sell it for a thousand worlds.' And Spurgeon's editorial comment was: She had just told me that she had not any hope of salvation, yet she would not sell it for a thousand worlds! In short, her instincts assumed what her words denied.

Now, that is what you see in this psalm. Here in the pit may be the clearest evidence that true faith dwells in you—in this knee-jerk reaction of faith. Do you catch it? After the despair of verses 1-2, you simply keep calling

'Yahweh, my God!' (v. 3a). You simply can't leave Him.
You must, then, be His.

Thirdly, we hear **the reasons faith marshals in
verses 3b-4**. Now note David's petition in these verses—
'Give light to my eyes.' We usually don't use expressions
like that, so it may seem a bit puzzling. But we have an
expression very like it back in 1 Samuel 14:29. There
Jonathan, King Saul's son, was going through a stretch
of woods while charging after Philistines. He happened
upon some honey there, stopped, and scooped some for
himself. Those with him were aghast, because King Saul
had placed the whole force under a curse should they eat
anything before he had gotten vengeance on the Philistines.
Jonathan's answer was that his father had simply made
trouble with that oath. See, he said, 'how my eyes lit up
when I tasted that bit of honey' (NJPS). He was referring to
the fresh surge of energy and stamina that a few calories
had given him. So, here in the psalm, David asks for
Yahweh to supply him with fresh strength and energy in
the face of the assaults and troubles he is enduring.

But after he prays, 'Give light to my eyes,' David piles
up these clauses—three of them—each beginning with
'lest.' (Actually in the Hebrew text the particle for 'lest'
only appears twice, but when it is written in the first line,
as in v. 4, it is meant to be 'carried over' in the second
line—hence a total of three 'lests' in our translation.)
What is he doing? He is supporting his petition with
arguments, bringing reasons to bolster his request, why
Yahweh should 'give light to my eyes.' The first argument,
he says, has to do with my fate—'lest I sleep in death' (3b);
the second, he would say, has to do with my shame—'lest

my enemy should say, "I have trounced him!"; lest my adversaries rejoice because I stagger' (4). Does Yahweh want his servant to meet his end (cf. Ps. 116:15) and see David's enemies celebrating his downfall? The argument probably implies that what will be David's shame would prove to be Yahweh's shame as well, for David's demise would imply Yahweh was unable (or unwilling) to deliver His servant.

But here in this psalm I am not so much concerned with the particular arguments David uses as with the fact that he uses arguments, reasons, in his petitions. For this implies, doesn't it, that prayer is a *thinking* exercise? There is a sense in which prayer should be so terribly logical and rational. Do you pray that way? Do you press reasons upon Yahweh as to why He should answer your plea? Can you make an argument for the petition you bring?

But I want to go beyond this as well. Take in the whole of the psalm so far and see what a *model of proper biblical piety* you meet here. Do you remember the despair and terror of verses 1-2—the sheer *emotion* there? Then you read verses 3-4 and you are caught in an argument, you are hearing *reasoning*. Do you see the combination? In verses 1-2, there is especially the feeling, in verses 3-4, the thinking; in the former, emotion, in the latter, reasoning; in 1-2, the affections are laid bare, in 3-4, the arguments are pressed. Not either-or, but both-and.

It all reminds me of something John Bright once wrote, just as an aside, in one of his books. He said that when he got dressed in the morning he did not need to decide whether to wear a shirt or trousers—rather the properly attired man wore both. David depicts a similar point here in Psalm 13. Sometimes in our Christian or church 'culture' we get pushed one way or the other— some urging us, if we think of extremes, to swing and sway to the beat and bounce of Roop-tee-do 'Songs of Praise' and others to furrow our brows and get into brain-cell Christianity. But the psalm implies that especially in prayer you must hold both emotion and reason together. In a true knowledge of God they combine. At the throne of grace, tears fall from your eyes and arguments from your lips.

Finally, David shows us in vv. 5-6, **the anchor faith holds**. Actually, he shows us more than that, but I will only deal with the turning point in verse 5a here, because I want to focus on what makes all the difference in David's trouble, what accounts for the 'turnaround' in these six short verses and why with his earlier despair he can be so confident of coming joy.

Pronouns are sometimes signals of turnarounds in the psalms, emphatic pronouns like we meet in the first part of verse 5: 'But I, I have trusted in your unfailing love.' Notice that David is not looking inward here. He is not saying that he has gotten a fresh shot of self-esteem or that he has begun to feel better about himself. No, he fastens on to Yahweh's character, he has latched on to His 'unfailing love.' That translates the word *ḥesed*. Now what is Yahweh's *ḥesed*?

You will run into a number of English translations for the word. The RSV and ESV use 'steadfast love,' the NASB 'lovingkindness,' others tend to use simply 'love' (e.g., NIV) or 'mercy' (cf. NKJV). The first matter you should remember about *ḥesed* is that it is a miracle. Perhaps you can recall Yahweh's self-description in Exodus 34:6—'Yahweh, Yahweh, a God compassionate and gracious, slow to anger, and rich in *ḥesed* and fidelity.' Remember when He said that? In the wake of Israel's apostasy and rebellion of Exodus 32, when they had worshiped the golden calf in the very shadow of Sinai. Moses had not even gotten down from the mountain with the covenant documents before they had already shattered the covenant. It was like a bride being married and then going to bed with someone else that night. So Moses went about interceding before Yahweh for this flaky bunch of rebels. It seems more than one could hope for that Yahweh would renew His covenant with such a batch of sinners. Yet He does, and part of the inexplicable reason is that He is 'rich in *ḥesed* and fidelity.' When you see *ḥesed* in light of Exodus 32–34, you have to say that *ḥesed* has no right to exist. The dregs of Israel had no reason to expect it. So *ḥesed* always seems to have a tinge of *grace* about it. It's faithful love that should not be, except that it's the way Yahweh is in the depth of His being, in His *ḥesed*-rich nature.

But *ḥesed* not only carries this notion of *surprise* but has overtones of *steadfastness* as well. You can sense it in some attempts to translate the word: 'steadfast love' or 'faithful love' or, here in Psalm 13, the NIV's 'unfailing love.' It is not merely love but loyal love, not merely kindness but dependable kindness, not merely affection but affection that has committed itself. It is not simply love but love that has 'stick-um' on it, love that refuses to ever let go. And so *ḥesed* has a sustaining, assuring element about it. 'If I say, "My foot slips," your *ḥesed*, Yahweh, holds me up'

(Ps. 94:18). But you have a far more familiar text than that to conjure up. Remember Psalm 23:6? You are familiar with 'goodness and mercy,' but the traditional 'mercy' there is actually *ḥesed*. So David says, 'Only goodness and *ḥesed* will pursue me all the days of my life.' It's almost a humorous picture. The verb 'pursue' ('follow' is too weak) is frequently used of enemies pursuing someone to do harm. But here David stands that verb on its head. He says he is so cared for that it's as if Yahweh has two special agents, Goodness and *ḥesed*, and these two Yahweh-commissioned agents stay in hot pursuit of David, always seeking to waylay him and heap more of God's kindness and goodness upon him! Do you see what *ḥesed* is in Psalm 23:6? It is the unguessable and lavish friendliness of Yahweh, with which He pledges to dog your tracks all your days.

What might it feel like to be the object of *ḥesed,* of faithful love? Here I often think of a story William Still (see his *Dying to Live*) tells of the earlier days of his pastorate in Aberdeen. He recalls a period when the dominant theme of his preaching seemed to be judgment and hell and the consequences of turning a deaf ear to the gospel. He kept hammering away at this (and he was convinced the Lord had led him to do so), but he knew it was getting the people down. Mr. Still had a dear aunt who served him as cook and housekeeper, and one Sunday at lunch during this hell-as-the-theme-du-jour period she voiced her concern. 'I am sitting there with them in the pew,' she said, 'and taking it all.' She went on: 'I feel for them. Oh, Willie, is there no love in the gospel?' Still admitted that her query had shaken him, but he responded that he could preach nothing but what the Lord had laid on his heart. 'Well,' his aunt replied, 'if it goes on, there will soon be no one there but you and me!' 'And will you desert me then?', Mr. Still asked. 'Never,' she shot back: 'I committed myself to you and the Lord's work here and I will never leave you.' That's *ḥesed*. And if you are not swallowed up by the darkness or swept away by the distress, it will be because in the midst of it all you have a God and Savior who says, 'I have committed myself to you and I will never leave you.' Just to be assured of unfailing love makes all the difference.

You may still be unsure whether you ought to pray prayers like this. Let's come at the matter in a back-door sort of way. Paul Johnson has an intriguing statement about Vladimir Lenin in his book *Modern Times*. 'He never visited a factory or set foot on a farm.... He was never to be seen in the working-class quarters of any town in which he resided.' But what does Lenin have to do with a psalm like this? Well, compare Paul Johnson's statement about Lenin with the way the writer of Hebrews depicts Jesus: 'In the days of his flesh, he offered up prayers and supplications, with loud cries and tears, to him who was able to save him from death, and he was heard for his godly fear' (Heb. 5:7). Jesus had no part in the stand-off, sanitized conditions Lenin evidently enjoyed. So don't be ashamed to pray these prayers. Jesus wasn't—He was right down here in the darkness, praying 'working-class' prayers like this. How dare you say that you are somehow above these cries!

Psalm 14

For the music leader. Of David.

(1) The fool has said in his heart, 'There is no God.'
They corrupt, they do abominable deeds;
there is no one doing good.

(2) Yahweh peers down from heaven upon the sons of man
to see whether there is anyone who understands,
who is seeking God.

(3) The whole lot has turned aside,
together they have become depraved;
there is no one doing good
—there is not even one.

(4) Do they not know—all the workers of wickedness,
who eat up my people (as) they eat bread?
They do not call on Yahweh.

(5) There they are terribly terrified,
for God is in the generation of the righteous.

(6) You want to put to shame the plans of the afflicted,
but Yahweh is his refuge.

(7) O that the salvation of Israel would come from Zion!
When Yahweh restores the fortunes of his people,
Jacob can rejoice, Israel can be glad.

2
Unfaith: From Fool to Fortress

We once had a dog named Sarah, and a fellow who claimed to know said he thought she was about six-eights beagle. (I never asked why he didn't reduce the fraction.) Dogs can be like that—a bunch of this and a little of that. In short, mongrels. And this is a mongrel psalm. Scholars like to identify psalms by their 'type,' but Psalm 14 baffles them a bit because they are not sure whether to call it a lament or a wisdom psalm or a prophetic exhortation or what. It doesn't easily fit any of our learned labels. It seems to be a bit of this and a snatch of that. How should one deal with a mongrel psalm? Same as with a canine mutt: love it, receive it, and—in the case of a psalm—listen to it. The message of the psalm is straightforward: *Mankind is universally depraved, yet there are a people who have been—and will be—delivered.* What then do we find as we move through this psalm?

Firstly, the psalm depicts **a corrupt people (vv. 1-3)**. Here is a particular case, a sample of humanity, the 'fool.'

The Hebrew word is *nābāl* (cf. 1 Sam. 25:25). You will find a thumbnail sketch of a *nābāl* in Isaiah 32:6, where it is clear that the mark of a fool is not intellectual deficiency but aggressive ungodliness. Here in our psalm the fool speaks—note the where and the what. He speaks 'in his heart,' so what he says may not be public; it could be secret. But if it is secret it is no less stubborn, for the heart is the controlling centre of a person. When he says in his heart 'There is no God,' that creed is what really drives his living and his thinking. Commentators sometimes say this is likely a practical atheism that is being brandished here (apparently there were few academic atheists in Israel). The fool means, then, that God does not matter, He does not count. And this creed has consequences: 'they corrupt, they do abominable deeds' (i.e., they corrupt in their influence/impact, following Allen Ross).

I think a brief tangent may be useful here. When we hear someone express their 'faith' in terms of denial ('There is no God'), I think we can easily suppose that such a person has thought profoundly about such matters and must have what seem to be rational grounds for his/her position. That is not necessarily the case at all; it may be sheer fear or prejudice that drives their 'faith.' John Blanchard, in one of his books, passes on the statement of Harvard scientist George Wald (a 1967 Nobel 'prizer'). Wald said that when it comes to the origin of life on earth, there are only two possibilities—creation or spontaneous generation. Spontaneous generation, Wald said, was disproved a hundred years ago, but that leads to only one other option, supernatural creation. 'We cannot accept that ... therefore we choose to believe the impossible, that life arose spontaneously by chance.' Not a very scientific way to arrive at truth. So don't be intimidated when someone wrinkles his forehead, bites his lip, narrows his eyes, and spouts the fool's creed. It can simply be his form of escapism.

But it's worse than we thought. Well, even in verse 1 David indicates by the plural verb forms ('they corrupt, they do abominable deeds') that he wasn't merely thinking of an isolated 'fool' here and there. But in verses 2-3 David clearly shows he is not thinking of a particular case but a universal condition—the whole race consists of *nābāls*!

> Yahweh [emphatic] peers down from heaven upon the sons of man
> to see whether there is anyone who understands,
> who is seeking God.
> The whole lot [emphatic] has turned aside,
> together they have become depraved;
> there is no one doing good
> —there is not even one (vv. 2-3).

There is no way of overturning this verdict. Yahweh Himself has checked it out thoroughly. The verb 'peers down' (*šāqap*) indicates close and careful scrutiny. It is the verb used of Sisera's mother in Judges 5:28 as she looks through the window, squinting and trying to catch a glimpse of her son's chariot returning. Verse 2, however, gives a different angle on the godlessness of men and women; verse 1 indicated such godlessness may be rooted in blatant denial ('there is no God'), but verse 2 shows it may be expressed in thoughtless neglect (no one 'is seeking God'). People simply have no desire for God, no longing to know and enjoy Him. A pastor can meet it in his study. Here is a couple who want to be married. The pastor asks them to tell him about their Christian faith. He hears nothing about their sense of their own guilt and need, nor of grateful delight in a crucified Savior. He hears something like this: 'Every once in a while when I have a bad day and am down, then I pray and things seem to get better.' In other words, God is my psychological genie and whenever I need a lift, I take him out and dust him off. That's human depravity in its more 'polite' form. But there is no hunger or thirst for God, no longing, no craving to have and to know Him.

So verse 3 gives the decided verdict: 'the whole lot has turned aside.' It is a blanket condemnation: 'there is no one doing good—there is not even one.' That last clause may be added lest you are tempted to swallow the nonsense that says the psalmist is using hyperbole, speaking in exaggerated terms in order to make a point. But 'there is not even one' undercuts that; it's as if he says, 'Now I want you to understand that this is true literally, individually, and exhaustively.' You, of course, may beg to differ about this morose assessment, but then you are not writing the psalm, are you? And we're trying to understand the psalm and when we follow its argument we find ourselves facing a crisis bar none.

Paul picks up on this 'crisis' in Romans 3:9-20. In that passage, Paul is arguing that 'Everyman,' whether religious man (Jew) or pagan man (Greek), is under the power of sin (v. 9), and to support his point he launches into a bunch of Old Testament quotations, beginning with Psalm 14:1-3 (Rom. 3:10-12). After this battery of Old Testament texts (which amount to an omni-biography of every man and woman) we come to verse 19, where

Paul says, 'Now we know that whatever the law [here he means the old covenant Scriptures] says, it speaks to those who are within the scope of the law.' What does he mean by that? Something like this: the Old Testament Scriptures are speaking to—and about—those who have received the Old Testament Scriptures. This damning series of texts in Romans 3:10-18 is describing Israelites. Well, a bit of thought tells us it must be that way with Psalm 14:1-3. When David spoke of the 'fool' in verse 1, he wasn't depicting a Moabite fool but a fool within the normal orbit of his sphere of life—an Israelite fool; when he speaks of those who have no taste for God in verses 2-3, he doesn't have Philistines in mind. He is referring to people within his usual purview—people in Israel. So Psalm 14:1-3 reflects the situation in Israel, among the professing people of God. No exemptions here. We like to cherish the thought that we may be exceptions. I suppose the contemporary counterpart might be someone who says, 'But I am a part of a Bible-believing, gospel-preaching fellowship.' Okay, but what is there about Psalm 14:2-3 that you don't understand? It is a snip of your biography.

Martyn Lloyd-Jones once told of his preaching at the 1941 mission at Oxford University. The first service was on a Sunday night and the congregation consisted chiefly of students. It had been announced that after the service there would be an opportunity to ask the visiting preacher questions; this gathering would be in another nearby building. So Lloyd-Jones preached. Afterwards he and the convener went to the question-time, neither apparently expecting more than a few. However, the place was packed. One bright and classy student in the front row said he had a question. After properly paying the preacher some compliments, he said that the sermon had raised a deep difficulty in his mind; it was that it seemed that Lloyd-Jones' sermon could have been preached just as well to a congregation of farm laborers or anyone else. He sat down, while the whole group roared with laughter. Lloyd-Jones replied that he was interested in the student's question but couldn't really see the questioner's difficulty, for, though he might be thought a heretic, he had to admit that up to that moment he had regarded undergraduates —and graduates as well—of Oxford University as being just ordinary, common human clay and miserable sinners like everybody else, and that their needs were the same as agricultural laborers or anyone else. The incident highlights the danger: we so flatter ourselves that we are somehow exceptions—and this psalm fully flattens such flattery.

If we accept the testimony of Psalm 14 then, how will it affect us? Maybe in our prayers. Arthur Bennett put together that collection of Puritan prayers called *The Valley of Vision* (Banner of Truth), and I find a number of them so refreshing because few folks pray like this anymore. For example:

> But in my Christian walk I am still in rags;
> > my best prayers are stained with sin;
> > my penitential tears are so much impurity;
> > my confessions of wrong are so many aggravations
> > > of sin...
> I need to repent of my repentance;
> I need my tears to be washed.

I never do anything else but depart from thee,
>> and if ever I get to heaven it will be because
>> thou willest it, and for no reason beside.

I am sinful even in my closest walk with thee;
it is of thy mercy I died not long ago....
My heart is an unexhausted fountain of sin,
>> a river of corruption since childhood days,
>> flowing on in every pattern of behaviour.

People who pray like that are people who believe the witness of this psalm about a corrupt people.

However, if you assent to verses 1-3, you find the psalm becomes a mystery and faces you with a conundrum. You meet, in the second place, **an unexplainable fact**. You begin to think as you read on, 'Well, if verses 1-3 are true, how is it that I read what I read in verses 4 and following?' What do I mean? Why, you read of 'my people' (v. 4), of the 'generation of the righteous' (v. 5), of 'the afflicted' (v. 6). You see the rub? You have the emphatic testimony of verses 1-3 and yet here Yahweh has someone He calls 'my people.' For all the across-the-board corruption of the race, there is yet a 'generation of the righteous.' How did God get these? Where did these come from? They are just there. There is then a silent assumption in this psalm—it forces you to posit the wonder of grace.

Perhaps this point comes to mind more readily in connection with New Testament texts, texts which may be more familiar and more explicit. Think of Ephesians 2:1-3. There Paul tells us what we were. We were *dead*, 'dead in our trespasses and sins' (v. 1). Corpses respond to nothing, least of all to the gospel. And we were *dominated*, both in an external way (we 'walked' in lockstep under the 'authority of the ruler of the air' [v. 2], hence as Satan's lackeys) and in an internal way (we conducted our lives 'in the lusts/desires of our flesh' [v. 3a], governed by our own God-rejecting nature). Even more, we were *damned*, for, as Paul says, 'we were by nature children of wrath' (v. 3b)—and Paul's 'we' may well mean 'we religious Jews' as well as godless pagans. So that is our 'bio'—we are lifeless, helpless, and hopeless. And then Paul writes those words that are too much to hope for: 'But God....' 'But God, who is rich in mercy' (v. 4)—why should He be like that? 'But God...made us alive together with Christ' (v. 5)—why should He do anything like that? Or take 1 Corinthians 6:9-11. Sometimes I like to read this text the very first thing in congregational worship, so that the very first words the people hear in worship are: 'Do you not know that the wicked will not inherit the kingdom of God? Do not be deceived: Neither the sexually immoral nor idolaters nor adulterers nor male prostitutes nor homosexual offenders nor thieves nor the greedy nor drunkards nor slanderers nor swindlers will inherit the kingdom of God.' Without missing a beat and with some 'punch,' one keeps reading: 'And that is what some of you were. But you were washed, you were sanctified, you were justified in the name of the Lord Jesus Christ and by the Spirit of our God' (NIV). Naturally, if that text is the 'call to worship,' the first hymn should immediately follow and it should be Isaac Watts' 'How Sweet and Awesome Is the Place,' in which the congregation sings:

> While all our hearts and all our songs
>   join to admire the feast,

each of us cries, with thankful tongue,
  'Lord, why was I a guest?

'Why was I made to hear your voice,
    and enter while there's room,
when thousands make a wretched choice,
    and rather starve than come?'

And so we confess what we might call the 'flabbergasting-ness' of the gospel.

In the annals of American college football, the 1979 Sugar Bowl game holds an honored place. The University of Alabama defeated Penn State 14-7. On the night after that Sugar Bowl victory, some Alabama loyalists were having a party in the suite of legendary coach Paul 'Bear' Bryant in the Hyatt Hotel. Coach Bryant had on a new T-shirt but it had a hole in it. One of the guests pointed out this malady to Bryant. The coach's response was, 'Yeah, I know. I always tear a small hole in my T-shirts so I'll never forget where I came from.' No matter what success and acclaim he received, Paul Bryant apparently felt it was vital that he never forget that he grew up on a hardscrabble farm in Arkansas, in a place that originally wasn't even on the state map—called Moro Bottom. And Christians must never forget where they came from, that they were 'children of wrath, like the rest of mankind,' having no hope and without God in the world (Eph. 2:3, 12).

Finally, David speaks of **a mighty fortress** (vv. 4-7). This last chunk of the psalm breaks down into three parts: (1) sympathy on the part of God (v. 4); (2) fallacy on the part of the wicked (vv. 5-6); and (3) expectancy on the part of God's people (v. 7).

Notice that verse 4 makes it clear that there is nothing theoretical or clinical about the universal depravity in verses 1-3, for it is expressed in assaults on God's people. Yahweh *has* a people and it is a *suffering* people. But what is astonishing is that Yahweh Himself 'breaks into' the psalm (at least in the first two lines of verse 4—note the first person 'my people') and what is astonishing is that Yahweh seems astonished over the callous cruelty inflicted on His people. 'Do they not know—all the workers of wickedness, who eat up my people (as) they eat bread?' The 'as' is not expressly in the text but seems implied. They swallow up my people, He implies, and think no more of it than scarfing down their lunch. The God who speaks like this is the amazing God the prophet describes in Isaiah 63:9—'in all their affliction he was afflicted.' Yahweh simply cannot stand to see the suffering of His people—and here in this psalm He laments it unashamedly.

Sadly, Psalm 14 is very current—the people of God are continually being swallowed up. During the summer in which I am writing this, in one region of an African country Muslims destroyed 43 Christian-owned farms. No one was arrested for this. But that wasn't enough. Two days later came attacks on nine Christian villages; dozens of people were killed. But that wasn't enough. The next day at the funeral for these victims, Muslims again attacked and gunned down, among others, two Christian politicians. But that wasn't enough. In less than two weeks, Islamist militants made attacks on twelve villages. Church members took refuge in the home of a local church leader—his house was bombed and more than 50 people were burned alive. Month after month, it is the same story, whether in Africa or the Middle East or Asia. 'They eat up my people as they eat bread.' It's not difficult at all.

But these butchers have miscalculated and made a fallacious assumption. They meet with something that they had not counted on—that these seemingly helpless people have a defender (vv. 5-6). 'There'—it does not say where, simply wherever it will occur—'they are in great terror' (ESV). I have tried to pick up the emphasis of the text with 'they are terribly terrified.' Why so terrified? Because they discover that God is both present with and protecting of His people. On the one hand, God is (literally) 'in the generation of the righteous' (v. 5) and He is the 'refuge' of the afflicted (v. 6). Apparently, they didn't see the sign that read: 'Beware of sheep.' You touch God's people and you will find yourself—sooner or later—having to deal with their God. The response of heaven to those crushing God's people is the terror of judgment. Yahweh delivers His people by judging and destroying their enemies.

And that forms the fervent hope of Yahweh's battered people—'O that the salvation of Israel would come from Zion!' That will be the time when Yahweh 'restores the fortunes of his people' (not, 'bring back the captivity,' as in NKJV), when every enemy will be liquidated and every danger eliminated, when He will set them in the safety for which they long (cf. Ps.12:5). That time may seem far down the pike, but there is no doubt about it. The text does not speak of some 'if' but of a 'when'— 'When Yahweh restores the fortunes of his people.' This final salvation is assumed to be certain; after the misery there will be mercy. That does not bring immediate relief but does provide a rock-ribbed certainty that sustains hope. We may be in the pit but this assurance of complete deliverance is God's way—in the meantime—of building a floor in the pit.

I think the most comforting piece in this 'fortress' section of the psalm comes from Yahweh's lament in verse 4: 'Do they not know—all the workers of wickedness, who eat up my people (as) they eat bread?' It is a combination of warm sympathy and irate indignation. If Yahweh is that distressed over the distress of His people, surely nothing will stop Him from putting things right for them. The words reveal all. I recall once hearing my father express his aggravation with an elder in the congregation. Apparently, this man had verbalized a patently false accusation against my father, and my father—looking back on that moment—exclaimed: 'It was only the grace of God that kept me from knocking him down!' Most Presbyterian pastors don't talk that way—at least out loud. But that my Dad did shows how intense his frustration and anger were. And Yahweh's words in verse 4 show both His exasperation with and His intentions for the 'workers of wickedness.' And therein rests the hope of a suffering people.

Well, it's not bad for a 'mongrel' psalm. It tells you that you are depraved, rescued, and secure, leaving you at last in the hands of your mighty Fortress. You could do worse than that.

Psalm 15

A psalm of David.

(1) Yahweh, who can sojourn in your tent?
     Who can dwell in your holy hill?

(2) The one who walks wholeheartedly,
        and practices righteousness
        and speaks truth in his heart.

(3) He does not go round slandering with his tongue;
     he does not do harm to his fellow man;
     and he does not speak derisively against his neighbor.

(4) In his view a rejected person is despised,
     but he honors those who fear Yahweh;
     he goes on oath to his own harm
        and does not change.

(5) He does not give out his silver at interest,
     and he does not take a bribe against the innocent.
     The one who keeps doing these things
        will never be shaken.

A Cure for Flippant Worship   3

Once when I was a wee lad we were visiting my
grandma in southern Kansas. She was actually my father's
stepmother but was the only grandma I ever knew. She
was a delightful lady and our whole family loved her. By
this time, my grandfather had died and grandma lived
alone. We were seated at a round table about to enjoy our
evening meal. A prayer of thanks was the next item on
the agenda. Now my father was a pastor, so he often was
chosen to 'ask the blessing' for food about to be devoured;
indeed, as I recall, grandma often asked my Dad to pray
before meals. But she had said nothing this evening as
we sat down and began to bow our heads in anticipation.
Okay, so I peeked—and I'm glad I did, because I captured
a 'frozen moment,' one of those delicious two seconds
when nothing happened and time stood still. I glimpsed
my father with his eyes clamped shut and mouth open,
ready to utter the required prayer. But before a syllable

became vocal, grandma started praying! That rendered my father's imminent effort redundant. Even though grandma had not specifically asked him, my father had assumed that—of course—he was to pray.

We too easily make unfounded assumptions like that. All too casually we may think of having fellowship with God. All too easily we may come to the next episode of public worship. And Psalm 15 stands in the way, like a blinking, yellow caution light at an intersection. Not so fast, it seems to say; how do you know you are one of the worshipers the Father is seeking to worship Him? (cf. John 4:23). Psalm 15 means to jolt us out of our overly-familiar 'of course' attitude toward Yahweh's worship. What then does Psalm 15 press upon us?

The psalm takes us right back to square one and makes us begin with **the question that matters** (v. 1):

> Yahweh, who can sojourn in your tent?
> Who can dwell in your holy hill?

There was a sort of double 'tent' and 'holy hill' in David's time. In 2 Samuel 6, David finally brought back the ark of the covenant to his new capital, Jerusalem, and worship took place there (see 1 Chron. 16:37-38). However, the tabernacle had been at Gibeon (about 5 miles Northwest of Jerusalem) for some time and so sacrificial worship occurred there (see 1 Chron. 16:39-40; 2 Chron. 1:3-5). David's primary concern here does not seem to be with the specific location but with what should occur there—worship and communion with Yahweh. Nor must we squeeze too much juice out of the verbs he uses. The verb 'sojourn' (*gûr*), for example, can convey the idea of a temporary or passing residence; yet, as Alexander Maclaren points out, David can also say, 'I want to sojourn in your tent forever' (Ps. 61:4), an expression that gives 'sojourning' a long life!

Perhaps, as Michael Wilcock notes (*Psalms 1–72*, 55), the term 'tent' gives us the most suggestive picture of the concern of this verse. It's an 'exodus' word, conjuring up the memory of constructing Yahweh's tent sanctuary in Exodus 25–40, the climax of the book of Exodus. At the end of the book, there is God's tent in the midst of Israel's tents, a testimony to His own deep desire—as if Yahweh simply cannot get close enough to His people. And here in verse 1 is a responsive appetite to that kind of God. Here is one who longs for the 'friendship' or 'intimacy' of Yahweh (Ps. 25:14) that ought to be enjoyed in the place of worship.

The opening line of this psalm stands in stark contrast to that of Psalm 14. There we were told that the fool says in his heart, 'There is no God.' There is one who dismisses God, but here (15:1) is one who desires God, who seems to think that nothing is quite so important as meeting the conditions for enjoying Yahweh's fellowship. Sadly, it is a priority we easily lose sight of.

A few years ago I read a news clip about a Boston orthopedic surgeon being suspended from practice. It was a case of back surgery, a spinal fusion procedure. Six hours into the spinal surgery, this surgeon told his colleagues in the operating room that he had to 'step out.' What was so urgent? He went to the bank to deposit his paycheck. Somehow the Board of Registration in Medicine seemed to think a back surgery more important than a bank deposit.

We tend to fall into a like trap. We lose sight of the fact that most of the matters we are most wound up about aren't really that important. Truth be told, our latest cyber toys, golf dates, bridge clubs, church committees, ballet lessons are all a bunch of pretty trivial clutter. Maybe it takes a one-liner from Psalm 15 to jolt us back into focus with the question that matters.

Secondly, the psalm answers the question of verse 1 with **the description that searches us** (vv. 2-5b). One may not readily see the grammatical pattern of this description in an English translation but it seems to be present:

3 positive activities (v. 2, use of Hebrew participles)
3 negatives (v. 3, negative + Hebrew 'perfect' verbs)
2 positives (vv. 4a and 4b)
2 negatives (vv. 5a and 5b; negative + 'perfect' verbs)

However, it will be more useful for our purposes simply to break down this description into broad categories, to see what it tells us about the one who can enjoy the friendship of the Lord.

Firstly, verse 2 tells us of his *tendencies*. Here is a broad, general characterization, the Hebrew participles indicating continuous action and implying that this is the way such a person typically functions. He is one who 'walks whole-heartedly,' the way Abraham was to live (Gen. 17:1, 'Walk in my presence and be wholehearted'). Some translations have 'blamelessly' (which does not mean 'flawlessly' or 'sinlessly'), but the root word means 'whole' or 'complete' and so 'wholeheartedly' is a better rendering. 'Walking wholeheartedly' refers to one's basic covenant loyalty to

Yahweh. And the rest of verse 2 fleshes out what 'walking wholeheartedly' involves both externally ('practices righteousness') and internally ('and speaks truth in his heart'). Folks can observe the one but not the other—the latter is open only to Yahweh's scrutiny. 'Speaks truth in his heart' stands in sharp contrast to the fool in 14:1, who says 'in his heart, "There is no God."' Here then is the tone of the life of Yahweh's worshiper: he lives out of heart surrender to Yahweh and both the external and internal aspects of his life are consistent with that commitment.

Verse 3 focuses on the prospective worshiper's *speech*, especially the restraint that seems to govern it, e.g., 'he does not go round slandering with his tongue.' The next line is more general perhaps ('he does not do harm to his fellow man'), but the final line zeroes in on speech once more ('he does not speak derisively against his neighbour'). The word I've translated 'derisively' is actually a noun, traditionally rendered 'reproach'; however, it connotes ridicule or mockery or derision. In 1 Samuel 17 this root (*ḥrp*) occurs six times (vv. 10, 25, 26 [twice], 36, 45) in the derision Goliath heaped upon Israel and Israel's God. Here in our psalm it means that one does not mock or ridicule others because of their conditions or circumstances. So this verse describes the would-be worshiper negatively (what he does not do) and socially and stresses his control, particularly in his speech. His tongue will neither slander nor scorn.

Next, we get a glimpse of the worshiper's *affections*: 'In his view a rejected person is despised, but he honors those who fear Yahweh' (v 4a). That is hardly politically correct. Everyone knows that in our time we are to have our noses in the dust before the spineless deity called Tolerance.

What is this about despising a 'rejected person'? Who is a rejected person anyway? The sense is likely 'one rejected by God.' And in light of Psalm 53:4-5 those whom God rejects are those who assault and seek to annihilate His people. That could well be the sense here in Psalm 15. Since the prospective worshiper honors those who fear Yahweh, one might assume that that is surely something a 'rejected person' would *not* do. This worshiper then has preferences, makes distinctions, has both affections for God's people and antipathy toward those who oppose them. Someone, of course, may raise and fly aloft the Matthew 7:1 flag here, as though we should have no part of making judgments or distinctions. But that won't wash. After Jesus' 'Judge not' dictum, He explains contextually that He is speaking of *hypocritical* judgment (Matt. 7:3-5), not of making judgments in general. Moreover, He then follows with: 'Don't give what is holy to dogs or toss your pearls before pigs' (Matt. 7:6, HCSB). If Jesus' command here means anything at all, it requires His disciples to make judgments, to discern. If one is to keep 'what is holy' from dogs and pearls from hogs, then one must be able to identify who the dogs and hogs are. Disciples are called to discriminate. I am only concerned to establish this principle here. (For exposition of Matthew 7:6, see D. M. Lloyd-Jones, *Studies in the Sermon on the Mount*, 2:183-94).

So...the would-be worshiper in Psalm 15 has decided affections—he despises and he honors. He has piety with an 'edge' to it. He is not some benign-feeling, neutrality-addicted glob. And such affections can be very revealing and reassuring, especially one's love and esteem for the Lord's people. Remember that dejected woman in Spurgeon's congregation at Waterbeach (see exposition of Psalm 13). She was forever doubting, convinced she was unconverted. Spurgeon asked her why she came to chapel if she believed she was a hypocrite and outside of Christ. Her response was: 'I come because I can't stop away. I love the people of God; I love the house of God; and I love to worship God.' Not likely then that she was unconverted. That's a good sign—if one loves the people of God with all their foibles and quirks.

Verse 4b underscores the worshiper's *integrity*: 'he goes on oath to his own harm and does not change.' The idea seems to be that such a person will keep his word even if it is not to his own advantage to do so. Modern situations can be very different; we don't always formally swear an oath. But imagine, for example, getting an estimate from a painter to have your house painted; you agree to give him the job. In the meantime you discover that a friend of a friend is willing to do the same work for substantially less. But you refuse to renege on your original commitment; you may be the loser financially but you are committed to keeping your word.

Finally, we meet the worshiper's *contentment* in verse 5ab. He doesn't lend money at interest (cf. Deut. 23:19-20); he is not concerned to bleed someone for as much as he can; nor—if he is in a legal position of some kind—does he take bribes in order to turn a case and nail the innocent with a guilty verdict. This is the same sort of integrity as in verse 4b. But it goes beyond that. Here is someone who is not obsessed by 'the economy,' who is not driven by covetousness or carried along by the contagion for 'more.' This is the sort of person who prays the prayer of Proverbs 30:7-9 and lets it go at that.

It was one man's contentment that so impressed John Wesley and inched him toward his conversion. Skevington Wood tells how Wesley had a conversation with the porter of his college late one night. Wesley found out that the man had only one coat and had nothing to eat or drink on that day except a little water. Still the man was full of gratitude to God. Wesley asked him, 'You thank God when you have nothing to wear, nothing to eat, and no bed to lie upon. What else do you thank Him for?' 'I thank Him,' the porter replied, 'that He has given me my life and being, and a heart to love Him, and a desire to serve Him' (*The Inextinguishable Blaze*, 100). Such contentment left its mark.

Now we must step back and take in this description (vv. 2-5b) as a whole. How are we to look at it? Derek Kidner is correct: this portrait is not an 'exhaustive catalogue.' We know this because not every detail would apply to every believing Israelite. Take the items in verse 5, for example. There were likely some Israelites so financially strapped that they couldn't dream of loaning money, let alone tacking interest on to it. There were others who had no civil or legal position and so would be in no place to be offered a bribe, let alone reject one. No, what we have here is more of a suggestive collage— but with enough specific details to keep us from taking refuge in mere warm, fuzzy feelings. Yet none of these 'marks' of a genuine worshiper are that extraordinary. These particulars are simply what ought to characterize any godly Israelite believer. In one sense, this almost four-verse description simply depicts genuine, faith-driven Old Testament piety.

However, it is helpful (because it may prove reassuring) to have this 'itemizing' of some of the features that typify an authentic worshiper of Yahweh. Recently I was reading the story of what I call the greatest motion picture ever made. I refer to *Hoosiers*, a 1986 American film about a small-town Indiana high school basketball team going all the way to the state championship. The setting is about 1952. One problem the film's originators faced was the pressure to film in Canada to save on costs; they insisted it must be shot in Indiana. Then the sets had to be right. There could be no signs indicating 'unleaded gasoline' since such wasn't sold in the early 1950s. Every store ad boosting Reebok tennis shoes had to be removed; the brand Reebok didn't exist then; Chuck Taylor All-Stars would be okay but not Reebok. Then the scenes of basketball action had to be carefully done: there could be no 'dunking' or dribbling between the legs, which are so common in basketball nowadays, for that was foreign to the 1950s' game. All that was done had to breathe authenticity, genuineness. That is the function of this detailed collage in the psalm: to show what an authentic, acceptable worshiper of Yahweh looks like. Since the text focuses on actions, we are kept from making feelings or emotions our index (though emotions and yearnings have their proper place; cf. Pss. 42:1-3; 84:1-2).

But some readers will not find these verses confirming but unnerving, for as they read through verses 2-5b they feel a cumulative weight building up and crushing them. As they mentally tick off each bit of this description they sense how far short they fall of these 'standards.' For them, reading of restrained speech, virile affections, unchanging integrity, or quiet contentment seems to conjure up a barrage of failure. It's as if the text has scratched a case of poison ivy and inflamed it all the more. These folks will say, 'Psalm 15 simply leaves me in tatters, in ruins.'

This is not the fault of Psalm 15. No one dare complain about there being 'no grace in this psalm.' Of course there is. Anything that brings you to your knees and shows you how pervasive your sin is and how much you need atonement and forgiveness is gracious. We should welcome having to say once more:

> Not worthy, Lord! to gather up the crumbs
> with trembling hand that from Thy table fall,
> a weary, heavy-laden sinner comes
> to plead Thy promise and obey Thy call.
>
> I am not worthy to be thought Thy child,
> nor sit the last and lowest at Thy board;
> too long a wand'rer and too oft beguiled,
> I only ask one reconciling word. (Edward H. Bickersteth)

So this description (vv. 2-5b) may be either reassuring or restorative. Either way it's a description that searches us.

Lastly, the psalm supplies us with **the assurance that settles (v. 5c)**: 'the one who keeps doing these things will never be shaken.'

Psalm 15 gives more than we expected. In light of verse 1, we might have expected verse 5c to read something like: 'the one who keeps doing these things will sojourn in God's tent, will dwell on his holy hill,' that is, will enjoy intimate communion with Yahweh. But 5c implies that there is more than was initially asked; these people (of verses 2-5b) not only enjoy God's presence (v. 1) but are kept in God's grip, and that continuously and permanently ('will never be shaken'). So we begin asking about communion and we end with security. This is so typical—what we call vintage Yahweh.

James McPherson, in his *Battle Cry of Freedom,* discusses the first significant battle in the War between the States, First Manassas (or, if you're a Northerner, Bull Run). It was a Southern victory and yet, as McPherson explains, it was more than a victory. For out of or in that battle Southern soldiers developed a bond of camaraderie and a confidence that they could win—in a word, a psychological boost that carried them well for two more years at least. There was a victory but there was more than a victory; there was an 'extra' that carried them along.

And this is so often the way with our covenant God. He has a way of breaking out beyond what we ask or imagine (Eph. 3:20). Here in the psalm we begin by wanting to sojourn in His tent and He concludes by assuring us that we are safe in His hand. Yahweh always gives more. Adoration is in order.

Psalm 16

A miktam. Of David.

(1) Watch over me, O God,
   for I have taken refuge in you.

(2) I have said to Yahweh,
      'You are my Lord,
         you are all the good I need.'

(3) [I have said] about the saints who are in the land,
      'They are the majestic ones,
      —all my delight is in them.'

(4) They multiply their pains—they buy into another (god);
   I will not pour out their drink offerings of blood,
   and I will not take up their names upon my lips.

(5) Yahweh is my allotted portion and my cup;
   you take charge of my lot.

(6) Measuring-lines have fallen for me in pleasant places;
   yes, a beautiful possession is mine.

(7) I will bless Yahweh, who has given me counsel;
   even in the night times my thoughts instruct me.

(8) I have set Yahweh before me always;
   because he is at my right hand I will never be shaken.

(9) Therefore my heart is glad and my glory rejoices
—even my flesh will dwell securely;

(10) for you will never abandon my life to Sheol
—you will never allow your favored one to see corruption.

(11) You will make known to me the path of life:
full joys in your presence,
pleasures at your right hand forever!

A Sheltered Life

4

We sometimes speak of 'a sheltered life' in a derogatory sense. We use the phrase of someone who has been pampered or who is naïve or inexperienced. Some fellow never learned to wash his own clothes or cook his own food because his mamma always did it for him till he was twenty-six. He has led a sheltered life. Older folks might use it of someone who has never had to use an outdoor privy, while younger people might think of someone who has never seen a drug deal. It's synonymous with someone who has had so much given to him or her, who has not had to struggle, who has had very few hard knocks. A sheltered life.

Psalm 16, however, speaks of the idea positively. And this doesn't mean David had few troubles. But in Psalm 16 there isn't quite that on-edge air of emergency as in other psalms of David. This psalm is more restful; here he ponders what anchors him, rather than what alarms him. 'Watch over me, O God, for I have taken refuge in you'

(v. 1). That is the 'sheltered life,' and in his meditation David commends it to you.

First, verses 1-4 tell us that the 'sheltered life' consists of **commitments**. And it begins with a commitment to yield submission to Yahweh as your supreme good (v. 2). David's words to Yahweh begin with 'You are my Lord,' that is, You're the boss. His next words are terse and a bit puzzling; 'my good not beyond you' would be one literal way of translating them. David seems to mean that he has no real good apart from Yahweh. I have paraphrased this as 'You are all the good I need.' One might call this the total 'commitment package': not only devotion ('You are my Lord') but also delight ('You are all the good I need'). This is what obedience to the first commandment (Exod. 20:3) should look like.

Thomas Brooks passed on a story about Bonaventure (d. 1274). The devil tempted Bonaventure, insinuating he was a reprobate and urging him to drink in the pleasures of this life since he was excluded from the future joys with God in glory. But grace was astir in Bonaventure and he answered, 'No, not so, Satan; if I must not enjoy God *after* this life, let me enjoy Him as much as I can *in* this life.' Bonaventure apparently knew God not only as supreme Lord but as 'exceeding joy' (Ps. 43:4), as the 'overflowing fountain of all good' (as the Belgic Confession puts it). That seems to be David's position in verse 2. In New Testament terms, we are not only speaking of knowing Christ but knowing the *surpassing worth* (Phil. 3:8) of knowing Christ. Here then David begins with the premier and yet most basic commitment: confessing his submission to God (2a) and confessing the sufficiency of God (2b).

This commitment, however, leads to another: it spills over into a commitment to find satisfaction in the people of God (v. 3). Of course, such an assertion depends on what verse 3 says or means, and it is a difficult text. Some think the 'holy ones' (my translation: 'saints') refer to angelic beings or to foreign deities. Suffice to say that since they are 'in the earth/land' it seems more natural to assume they are human and refer to God's people. I assume that the verb from verse 2 does double duty for verse 3 and so 'I have said' is to be understood at the opening of verse 3 as well. Though the rest of verse 3 has its difficulties, I believe my rendering (along with that of a number of English versions) carries the sense: 'they are the majestic ones—all my delight is in them.'

Verse 3, then, is the proper corollary of verse 2; the psalm assumes that if you delight in God, you will delight in His people. It's a biblical axiom. Think of Paul's passing statement in Colossians 1:4; we heard, he says, 'of your faith in Christ Jesus and of the love you have for all the saints.' Faith in Christ, love for saints, the vertical and the horizontal that always go together. Faith in Christ simply spills over into love, care, and esteem for His people.

You may think this point reeks of soft-headed idealism. But the Bible is quite realistic; it knows that the 'saints' do not always act saintly. A quick read of the New Testament epistles easily supports this contention. And it's true that the folks who sometimes infuriate, aggravate, and frustrate you the most are fellow believers. In fact, some churches seem to have self-appointed whiners who perpetually point out how hurtful and uncaring the particular fellowship is. But it's a bit like one's own children: they often have teeth missing, runny noses, and dead toads in their pockets; yet one wouldn't trade them for anything because of whose they are. So with the psalm; it won't let you off the hook: if Yahweh is your Lord (v. 2), you will prize his people (v. 3). Otherwise, something's wrong.

One could also say there's a third commitment, a sort of 'reverse' commitment to practice separation from godlessness and paganism (v. 4). Once more the Hebrew text is difficult in the first line of verse 4. He speaks of those who multiply sorrows for themselves should they 'acquire' or 'buy into another.' One assumes he refers to another god or deity. In any case, in the rest of verse 4 David rejects the lure of paganism. He refuses to pour out their 'drink-offerings of blood.' Did pagan rites perhaps involve ritual drinking of sacrificial blood? Nor will he take up the names of these rival deities on his lips in praise or prayer. So a commitment to the Lord (v. 2) and His people (v. 3) means a repudiation of any other worship or discipleship; it requires an exclusive commitment to Yahweh and His people. Of course, if you do this in our day you do the unthinkable—you turn your back on religious pluralism.

People seem to have an allergy to such either-or positions. Paul Boller tells of an incident when North Carolina Senator Zebulon Vance was on the campaign trail. Someone asked him where he stood on the issue of Prohibition. Vance replied, 'I will reply to the gentleman's question by saying that my head is strongly inclined to the great policy of prohibition, but my stomach yearns the other way. I may say therefore I truthfully declare myself as being divided on the issue' (*Congressional Anecdotes*, 115). Such a both-and policy often works well in politics but is a disaster in faith. It is the way to multiply pains and sorrows (v. 4a). So the properly sheltered life begins in a commitment that finds its good solely in Yahweh, that clings gladly to Yahweh's people, and that intentionally repudiates all other worship. That is how you must dig yourself in; that is where you must plant yourself.

In verses 5-7, we meet a second mark of the sheltered life: **contentment**. This contentment flows from a *satisfaction* David finds in Yahweh (vv. 5-6) and from the *direction* he receives from Yahweh (v. 7).

The picture in 5a may reflect one's daily provisions: 'Yahweh is my allotted portion and my cup.' It's as if he says, Yahweh Himself is my food and drink; He is the one who sustains and refreshes me. Here is a text the Christian can take to the communion table! Then the picture seems to change and depicts how Yahweh orders David's circumstances (vv. 5b-6): the words 'lot' (or 'allotment'; cf. Josh. 14:2; 15:1; 16:1; 17:1), 'measuring-lines' (and then the turf the measuring-lines enclosed; cf. Josh. 17:5, 14), and 'possession' (or, 'inheritance'; cf. Josh. 13:33) are often used in connection with dividing up the land of Canaan among the various tribes of Israel. Here David uses these terms in grateful acknowledgment of Yahweh's providence in ordering, marking out, and settling the circumstances of his life, in spite of its many 'dangers, toils, and snares.' Both Yahweh's sustenance (5a) and Yahweh's sovereignty (5b-6) completely satisfy him.

But David's contentment also comes from the direction he receives from Yahweh: 'I will bless Yahweh, who has given me counsel; even in the night times my thoughts instruct me' (v. 7). How does Yahweh give him counsel?

Through His written word. The very first psalm implies this: there the believer walks away from the *counsel* of the wicked (1:1) and instead meditates on Yahweh's torah (law, instruction) day and night (1:2). In Psalm 107:11 the 'words of God' are synonymous with the '*counsel* of the Most High,' and in Psalm 119:24 Yahweh's testimonies are called 'my *counselors*.' So Yahweh's counsel comes through His written word—and that seems to spill over into the 'night times' (v. 7b). Allen Ross suggests that 'night times' conjures up the activity that may occur at night, namely, meditation on God and His Word (see, e.g., Pss. 63:6; 77:6; 119:55, 148). Literally, the end of verse 7 reads, 'even in the night times my kidneys instruct me.' David does not mean that kidneys are educators—he uses the term to refer to one's conscience or deepest thoughts. Verse 7 then depicts a process: Yahweh gives counsel through His Word and the believer takes that word and ponders and 'chews' on it even, or especially, during the night, and finds that it becomes instruction and warning for him/her.

You may not appreciate how this direction from Yahweh produces contentment until you remember what it's like to be without such direction. A quarter-hour spent with King Saul in 1 Samuel 28 should help. Note there the utter misery and hopelessness of the king, and all of that comes from being cut off from any direction and guidance from God (vv. 6, 15). What a privilege to have Yahweh's counsel, to appropriate it and cogitate on it in your soul, and to discover His light then shines on your way even in the night times!

Now please note that David is not simply describing his contentment here; he is rather praising Yahweh for His gift of contentment. Verses 5-7 are the language of delight and acknowledgment and praise: Yahweh Himself satisfies him (5a) and also graciously orders all his affairs (5b-6) and provides all the direction he needs (7). Yahweh then is to be 'blessed' for this (7a). Andrew Bonar understood this. Graham Scroggie tells us that on the first Sunday after his marriage to Isabella Dickson, Dr. Bonar, combining sincere praise and subtle humor, gave out in church these lines to be sung:

> Unto me happily the lines
>   in pleasant places fell;
> Yea, the inheritance I got
>   in beauty doth excel.

Obviously, a lovely and congenial wife is not the whole of the beautiful 'inheritance' the Lord may give. But she may be part of it—and there are some of us who fancy ourselves the Lord's servants who can begin our praise precisely on that point. Sometimes the Lord satisfies us by giving us someone who herself satisfies us.

Thirdly, the sheltered life consists of **confidence** (vv. 8-11), a confidence that even stares death in the face and feels secure. David expresses his confidence in a general way in verse 8, as he speaks of his own resolution and of God's 'position.'

We might wonder exactly what he means when he says, 'I have set Yahweh before me always' (v. 8a). It brings to mind something that theologian Charles Hodge said about his childhood:

> As far back as I can remember, I had the habit of thanking God for everything I received, and asking him for everything I wanted. If I lost a book, or any of my playthings, I prayed that I might find it. I prayed walking

along the streets, in school and out of school, whether playing or studying. I did not do this in obedience to any prescribed rule. It seemed natural. I thought of God as an everywhere-present Being, full of kindness and love, who would not be offended if children talked to him (A. A. Hodge, *The Life of Charles Hodge*, 13).

It seems to me that that is a pretty good child-level description of 'setting the LORD always before me' (cf. NIV). It at least means I commit all things to Him and bring all things before Him.

But David not only speaks of his resolution but of God's nearness: 'because he is at my right hand I will never be shaken' (v. 8b). So we have this general expression of confidence here; as if David says, I come near to God and God is near to me—so I will never be shaken. Then verses 9-11 unpack in more detail what is involved in that 'never be shaken.' These verses spell out what 'never be shaken' means for the long term—dogged preservation in spite of death (vv. 9-10) and lasting pleasures in God's presence (v. 11).

Let's pick apart what we find here. David rejoices in what we would call whole-person security: 'Therefore my heart is glad and my glory rejoices—even my flesh will dwell securely' (v. 9). There is an obvious emphasis on 'even my flesh.' This security, he says, covers my physical being. But *why* is even his physical being secure? Note verse 10 begins with a causal connector: '*For* you will never abandon my life to Sheol [the realm of the dead]—you will not allow your favored one to see corruption' (For the rendering 'corruption' rather than 'pit,' see Bruce K. Waltke, *An Old Testament Theology*, 894-5). David is confident about even physical preservation; he appears convinced that though he may go to Sheol he will not be forever abandoned there.

But the New Testament preachers, Peter and Paul, say that this psalm is not merely about David—they quote Psalm 16 (especially verse 10) as speaking of the resurrection of Messiah Jesus (Acts 2:24-32; 13:34-37). Some scholars would say that there is nothing like that in Psalm 16 itself; they would say there is nothing of life beyond death there nor any reference to the Messiah. So how do the New Testament preachers find the Messiah in Psalm 16 if He is not there? Some would allege there is a 'double meaning' in Scripture and so New Testament preachers came to see a further meaning that the text did not originally have. It may sound impressive, but it really amounts to pulling a messianic rabbit out of a non-messianic text.

That is not the super-interpretation the apostolic preachers practiced. Look at Peter's exposition in Acts 2:29-31. He is acutely aware of the interpretive difficulties. If Psalm 16:10 refers to David it is manifestly not true, for, as he so much as said, 'David did die; he did rot; there's his tomb, and if you want to pay the tourist fee, you can see it.' So Peter makes an explicit *argument* to show how at least this verse (v. 10) of the psalm cannot apply solely to David. For one thing, Peter reminds us that when we think of David, we are not merely dealing with individual David but with dynastic David, for Yahweh had sworn an oath that He would set one of David's line on his throne (Acts 2:30; Pss. 89:3-4; 132:11). We must not then think of David as an isolated individual but as a covenantally connected one, who carries his promised royal Descendant, as it were, wrapped up with him. And since David was also a prophet (Acts 2:30a, 31; cf. 2 Sam. 23:1-2), he predicted the resurrection of the Messiah in Psalm 16:10.

But can one find a basis for any of this in Psalm 16 itself? I think the psalm points this way. For one thing, note the pattern of parallelism in the psalm. We have likely heard someone mention 'synonymous' parallelism when speaking of Hebrew poetry, referring perhaps to a couplet in which both lines say essentially the same thing. Like Psalm 12:2 ('Empty talk is what they speak, each one, with his neighbor; with smooth talk, with a double heart they speak') or Psalm 6:1 ('Yahweh, don't rebuke me in your wrath! Don't chasten me in your hot anger!'). But often the parallelism is not so parallel; often it can be what we might call 'additional' or 'supplemental.' In this scheme, the parts of a verse follow a pattern of 'it's-not-only-this-it's-also-this,' that is, the following line adds a 'what's more' to the preceding line. This pattern pervades Psalm 16. Let me paraphrase a few examples:

4b   I won't pour out their drink offerings of blood,
        and I won't even take their names up on my lips.

5   Yahweh is not only my allotted portion and my cup
        —he also takes charge of my lot.

6   The measuring-lines have fallen for me in pleasant places
        —in fact, my whole possession is beautiful.

7   I will bless Yahweh who counsels me,
        But I even get instruction and warning
           in the night times.

8   I have set Yahweh always before me,
        but he also stands at my right hand...

9   It's not only my heart and my glory that rejoice,
       but even my physical frame has security.

What does this mean for verse 10? It means that David is not simply repeating himself in the second line of the verse but saying something 'in addition.' Interpreters too easily assume that 'my soul' (or, 'my life') in 10a is equivalent to 'your favored one' in 10b. But this may well ignore the 'what's more' pattern in the psalm. Further, there is a reference pattern in the psalm that seems to be broken in 10b. We could start with verse 9 but why not go all the way back to verse 5 and track it? Note: 'my allotted portion,' 'my cup,' 'my lot' (v. 5); 'my kidneys' (lit., v. 7); 'my right hand' (v. 8); 'my heart,' 'my glory,' 'my flesh' (v. 9); 'my soul/life' (v. 10a)—then 'your favored one' in verse 10b. This will not convince the unconvinced but it's a bit striking to go through a whole raft of 'mys' and then suddenly get hit with a 'your' in 10b (with not even a conjunction before the clause—the ESV inserts 'or,' but it's not in the Hebrew). One might then be pardoned for thinking that 'your favored one' (ḥāsîd) may refer to someone related to but yet distinct from David himself. And Yahweh will never allow this favored one to see (i.e., experience) corruption and decay. So Peter's interpretation (Acts 2:29-31) seems perfectly consistent with Psalm 16 itself. Which shouldn't surprise us—we know where he got it (Acts 1:3).

If God's Favoured One will not see decay, if He triumphs over death, then of course all Messiah's people can have assurance of victory in the face of death. And that victory even reaches to our 'flesh' (v. 9b), for God will not abandon us to Sheol but will bring us along with Jesus in resurrection (1 Thess. 4:14). The text says to those sharing David's faith: because Yahweh is at your right hand you will never be shaken, and that means never shaken by death, because Yahweh's Favoured One has conquered it.

Seymour Hersh tells how there was quite a brouhaha in the Kennedy administration in 1960, when JFK accepted Lyndon Johnson as his Vice-Presidential running mate. There were many in the Kennedy network who were not Lyndon lovers. But John Kennedy mollified one of his aides with: 'I'm forty-three years old. I'm not going to die in office. So the vice-presidency doesn't mean anything.' What a terribly presumptuous (because so arrogant) and pitiful (because so short-sighted) sort of hope that was. Far better to have confidence in a risen Savior who has already tackled that trauma (Heb. 2:14-15). A sheltered life, then, is not a shameful but a marvelous matter—if your life is sheltered in Yahweh, your portion in life, your deliverer in death.

Psalm 17

A prayer. Of David.

(1) Hear, Yahweh, a righteous plea;
     pay attention to my cry;
     listen to my prayer
         —not uttered with deceitful lips.

(2) Let my vindication come forth from your presence;
     your eyes will look (on things) rightly.

(3) You have tested my heart;
     you have scrutinized (me) at night;
     you have refined me;
     you find nothing.
     I have determined that my mouth will not transgress.

(4) As for the deeds of man,
     by the word of your lips I have kept from the ways of the
     violent;

(5) my steps keep holding to your paths;
     my feet will not be shaken.

(6) I, I call on you,
         for you will answer me, O God;
     bend down your ear to me;
     hear my word.

(7) Make your acts of grace obvious,
     O Savior of those seeking refuge
          from adversaries at your right hand.

(8) Protect me as the apple of the eye;
     hide me away in the shadow of your wings,

(9) from the wicked who have wasted me,
     my enemies who eagerly close in on me.

(10) They are closed up (in) their prosperity;
     with their mouth they have spoken arrogantly.

(11) As for our steps, they have now surrounded us;
     they set their eyes to throw us on the ground.

(12) His likeness—like a lion that longs to tear apart,
     and like a young lion lurking in secret places.

(13) Rise, Yahweh!
     Confront him!
     Bring him down!
     Rescue my life from the wicked with your sword,

(14) from men by your hand, Yahweh,
     from men of (this) age,
     with their portion in (this) life;
     and with your treasure you fill their belly;
     they are satisfied with sons,
     and they shall leave their riches to their children.

(15) I, in righteousness I will see your face;
     I will be satisfied when I awake with seeing your form.

5

PRAY WITHOUT CEASING

Charles Hodge, who taught at Princeton Seminary for many years, was in his mid-thirties when an aggravation in the thigh of his right leg nearly reached breaking point. The pain was severe, the effort at walking unbearable. He endured a raft of treatments that medical skill and probably quackery at the time (ca. 1833) had devised. He was flat on his back on a couch with his leg frequently in a splint for well over two years. So…he met and taught his classes in his house from his couch; he wrote articles and reviews and edited a journal from his couch; he wrote his commentary on Romans on his back on his couch. Amazingly, nothing kept him from working; no matter his condition, he simply kept on working anyway.

Psalm 17 is a bit like that. It is a translator's minefield, but the overall structure is clear and looks like this:

Petition, vv. 1-2
    Defense of fidelity, vv. 3-5

Petition, vv. 6-9
    Description of enemy, vv. 10-12
Petition, vv. 13-14
    Expectation of faith, v. 15

Now it is true that the whole psalm is a prayer (see the heading) but not all of it consists of direct petition. David begins with an explicit petition (1-2) and then defends his integrity (3-5), makes another petition (6-9) and depicts his opponents (10-12), comes back to another petition (13-14) and expresses his confidence (15). What I want you to see is how David keeps coming back to petition—with all his other concerns he simply won't let go of it. With a Charles Hodge-like tenacity he simply won't let anything keep him from his 'work' here—to press his request upon Yahweh. And so Paul's command, 'Pray without ceasing' (1 Thess. 5:17), seems a suitable caption for Psalm 17.

Pray without ceasing in view of your integrity (vv. 1-5). David begins with a plea to be heard: literally, 'Hear, Yahweh, righteousness' (v. 1a). He closes the psalm with the same key word, righteousness (v. 15). Here in verse 1 he speaks of a righteous plea, in verse 15 of a righteous position. So David begs Yahweh to hear (v. 1); he wants Yahweh to show him to be in the right (v. 2a); and he is sure Yahweh will indeed look on his situation rightly (v. 2b). That is his petition—and then he includes a self-assessment; he argues for his own integrity (vv. 3-5).

Focus on the content of what he says in verse 3-5. He claims that God will find *no secret wrongs* (3a-d); God has searched him out, tested his heart. There is no hidden hypocrisy. He says there is *no verbal trespass* (3e; see also

1d). He has been very careful to control his speech and watch his words. And there has been *no overt defection* (vv. 4-5). He refers here to his public life, to what we may call his way and his 'walk'; and he insists that he shuns the ways of the violent and presses on in the paths of God. This is not due to his own unaided skill—it happens 'by the word of your lips' (4b).

Verses 3-5 give some readers a case of the jitters. They fear David is 'tooting his own horn' here, perhaps stroking and polishing up his own righteousness. Psalm writers are aware that there is a sense in which no one can stand up to the full blaze of God's scrutiny (see Pss. 130:3; 143:2). But David is playing in a more minor key here. He is not claiming sinlessness but steadfastness; he is not boasting of his perfection but arguing for his consistency; he is saying he has been loyal, not impeccable. Such consistency is important, of course, in its own right.

Willie Mays was an all-star centerfielder for the New York (later San Francisco) Giants mainly in the 1950s-60s. During part of his baseball career he played under a team manager who was a professing Christian, one who was verbal about his faith. This manager was a bit of an oddity because he didn't even use liquor or tobacco. But his team knew that he, a married man, was carrying on an affair with an airline flight attendant. Willie Mays said that not only did that manager not win anyone to his faith but no one took him seriously when he might talk about it. They thought consistency was crucial.

That is the assumption here as well. All very well for David to cry for Yahweh's help (vv. 1-2) but that praying must come from a life marked by a full-orbed fidelity to Yahweh, a life without those inconsistencies that turn a profession into a lie. Psalm 66:18 understands this: 'If I regard iniquity in my heart, the Lord will not hear' (NKJV). The Lord must hear. And my own life must not become a barrier to that 'hearing.' This then should lead me not to morbid introspection but to a candid self-examination (vv. 3-5), to be sure there is a 'togetherness' about my life, an integrity, which in turn encourages me to expect to meet a hearing God.

Secondly, the psalm instructs you to **pray without ceasing in view of your emergency (vv. 6-12)**. Once more we meet an explicit petition (vv. 6-9), then a description of the enemy (vv. 10-12). Let's focus on the petition for a moment.

Note what his petition tells you about Yahweh: (1) He is the God who pays attention: 'I, I call on you, for you will answer me, O God' (v. 6a); everything depends on that; if God does not hear, we may just as well close up shop; and (2) He is the God who repeats history (vv. 7-8). Let's flesh this out a bit.

The main verb in the traditional Hebrew text in verse 7a is one used three times in the plague narratives in Exodus (Exod. 8:22; 9:4; 11:7). It occurs in connection with the fourth (flies), fifth (livestock), and tenth (firstborn) plagues and means 'to make a distinction.' For example, in Exodus 8:22 (v. 18 in Hebrew), Yahweh promises He will make the land of Goshen distinct during the fourth plague—there may be flies all over Egypt but not on Israel's turf. Yahweh will make obvious His special care for Israel in sparing them. Hence my translation of verse 7a in this psalm: 'make your acts of grace obvious.' As if to say,

'Show yourself to be the exodus God again and set me apart by making me the clear object of your special care.'

The imagery in 8a adds to this picture: 'Protect me as the apple of the eye' (lit., 'as the little man, the daughter of the eye,' referring to the pupil of the eye). This language seems to pick up Deuteronomy 32:10, which depicts Yahweh's care for Israel in the wilderness:

> He found him in a desert land,
>> and in the howling waste of the wilderness;
> he encircled him, he cared for him,
>> he kept him as the apple of his eye (ESV).

Those who make occasional visits to the ophthalmologist understand this. How hard it is to keep one's eye open for those drops of dilating fluid! How easily we flinch. The eye is so vital and so sensitive that we are extra-protective of it. Yahweh's protection of Israel in the wilderness was vigilant and 'extra-careful' (we might even say 'touchy,' in the right sense) like that—and David asks that Yahweh would, as it were, repeat that history in his own case.

In verses 10-12, David launches into a description of the enemy that has a direct connection with his petition in verses 6-9, for it shows how *urgent* his petition is, that there is no time for delay. In fact, the last part of his petition, verse 9, already emphasizes the urgency when it refers to the wicked 'who have wasted me' and enemies 'who eagerly close in on me.' Desperation is the name of the game. David portrays his enemies in terms of their *insolence:* 'they are closed up (in) their prosperity; with their mouth they have spoken arrogantly' (v. 10). The first clause is difficult to translate, but the second clearly indicates their posture—the disdain and contempt they express. Then David points out their *intent:* 'they set their eyes to throw us on the ground' (v. 11b). Nothing less than inflicting complete ruin is their design. Finally, David provides an *image* of them: 'like a lion that longs to tear apart, and like a young lion lurking in secret places' (v. 12). Bluntly, their passion is for blood and guts, and one never knows when the assault will come. This sort of emergency (vv. 10-12), then, fuels the urgency of his petition (vv. 6-9). Indeed, that urgency simply explodes in the first part of verse 13: 'Rise, Yahweh! Confront him! Bring him down!'

Now it may sometimes be difficult for us as psalm-readers to possess the same intensity as Psalm 17 reflects. I, for example, am not the covenant king under imminent assault as, apparently, David was. And, though the Lord's saints, no matter where they live, seem to be a people beset with troubles, there are yet a number of them, perhaps especially in the West, who could honestly say that by God's grace and mercy they have not yet faced the dire kind of hostility and hatred depicted in this psalm. No need to take on guilt over that. But it may be an invitation to prayer. Let's go on a brief tangent.

In 1 Kings 17, Yahweh miraculously provides daily bread for a Phoenician widow, her son, and Elijah during a famine. Every day her jar and jug yield enough flour and oil for a ration of pancakes. Then her lad becomes ill and dies. In her anguish, she accuses Elijah of bringing up her iniquity for God's judgment, so that her son was put to death (v. 18). Elijah does not enter into a debate on sin and suffering; he takes her son up to his room, and begins to pray: 'Even against this widow with whom I am sojourning have you brought disaster by putting her son to death?' (v. 20). Do you see how Elijah prayed? He took up the widow's own words in verse 18 and essentially passed them on to Yahweh. As if he puts himself in her place and pleads from her point of view. So, we can put ourselves as it were in the position of others and plead their anguish before God for them.

I suggest we can use Psalm 17 this way. We ourselves (some of us, at least) may not be in the thick of a verses 6-12 situation. Yet at the present time Christians in Syria are there. So-called freedom fighters do not think freedom includes Christians; so thousands of Christians have had to abandon homes, employment, and churches to go where they can to obtain a hoped-for sliver of security. Or there are Nigerian Christians dying by the scores under the bombings, burning, and butchery of the Boko Haram terrorists. Or what of a Christian woman in south Sudan hoping against hope that the bombers of north Sudan will not fly over to massacre helpless civilians? If our trouble is not so severe, we can nevertheless vicariously adopt the position of our brothers and sisters and pray verses 6-12 to God on their behalf.

Finally, you are to **pray without ceasing in view of your expectation (vv. 13-15)**.

I have already alluded to verse 13. It begins the third direct petition of the psalm. David possibly has the ringleader of his opponents in view in verse 13: he refers twice to 'him' and the term 'wicked' is singular here. But in verse 14 his enemies clearly take in others, as he speaks of 'men…men of (this) age.'

As he sketches his opponents in verse 14, he is setting them up as a contrast with himself (in v. 15). But verse 14 is very difficult, as a comparison of English versions may suggest. The NIV, for example, takes the last half of the verse as describing God's people rather than David's opponents. I can't go into an involved discussion here. Suffice to say I think it better to take all of verse 14 as descriptive of David's enemies (see my translation; so too NKJV and ESV). They are 'men of this age,' 'their portion is in this life,' and they are men who have been on the receiving end of the goodness of God! He has, for instance, given them families and they have estates that they can pass on to their children. They may not see beyond their own portfolio but actually they have been bountifully blessed by what we call the common grace of God—though they are trying to annihilate God's servant. Luke 16:25 provides a fitting caption for their lives: 'remember that in your lifetime you received your good things' (NIV).

Beginning with an emphatic 'I' in verse 15 ('I, in righteousness I will see your face'), David draws a sharp division between himself and these 'men of this age' in verse 14—and between the scope of their hope and his own. Their horizon is this age and this life; his centers on seeing Yahweh's face and form 'when I awake.'

What 'time' does David mean by this phrase? I think he refers to 'awaking' post-death. The image of sleep can often be used of death (e.g., Job 3:13; Ps. 13:3) and one might 'awake' to restored life (cf. 2 Kings 4:31) or in a resurrected state (Isa. 26:19; Dan. 12:2). Mention 'resurrection' and some Old Testament scholars break out in hives. Perhaps you've run into their typical mantra in some Old Testament handbooks: that the Israelites were sort of brick-headed folks who never thought much about the afterlife, that what mattered to them was life now, and that those hints of hope we find in some Old Testament texts developed very late. But Israelites had to think about life post-death. The psalms themselves come from worshipers who are often hanging on by a thread, facing enemies who are only too glad to usher them through the gates of Sheol. And their hope need not be worked out in some carefully crafted doctrine. However, their testimony shows that they anticipated life with Yahweh beyond death (even in the land (!), Ps. 37:27-29; see also Pss. 49:14-15; 73:23-26; cf. 71:20). And here in 17:15 David contrasts himself to the this-world orientation of the people in verse 14, so that his 'when I awake' naturally points beyond this age.

I should also touch on a matter of translation since it affects what David may be expecting. Our text is often rendered, 'I will be satisfied...with your likeness' or 'in your likeness' (cf. ESV, NASB, NKJV). This may look to the transformation he expects to experience (cf. 1 John 3:2). However, I think—as sometimes occurs in poetry—that the verb 'to see' in 15a is meant to do double-duty and is meant to be supplied also in 15b. Hence I translate: 'I will be satisfied...with seeing your form' ('form' and 'likeness' may translate the same word, *tĕmûnâ*).

When we take the text this way, it reminds us of Moses—and of Miriam and Aaron. Do you remember how in Numbers 12 Miriam and Aaron raised all that flak against their younger brother Moses? Part of their yammering focused on how Yahweh had spoken through them and not through Moses alone (Num. 12:2). But Yahweh soon brought them up short, essentially saying that there was no one like Moses for either responsibility or privilege;

Moses was in a class all by himself. When Yahweh speaks to Moses, He doesn't use his usual ways of communicating with prophets, that is, by visions or dreams. 'I speak with him mouth to mouth, plainly, and not in riddles, and he looks upon the form of Yahweh' (Num. 12:8). 'Mouth to mouth' is very like face to face in Exodus 33:11: Yahweh 'used to speak to Moses face to face, as a man speaks to his friend' (ESV). This did not mean Moses 'saw' Yahweh in a 'bare-faced' way (Exod. 33:20); but it does mean that no one enjoyed the same level of intimacy and clarity as Moses the mediator did. So Moses looked on 'the form of Yahweh.'

Are David's words perhaps a deliberate spin-off of Moses' experience in Numbers 12:8? We might think of a three-year-old lad who has a big brother who plays college football (I am thinking of the American variety with the pointed ball). And one morning this wee fellow has got hold of his brother's game jersey with maybe a big number '55' on it. He puts it on, it drags on the floor behind him, the sleeves do the same at his side, he can hardly keep from tripping. One could probably wrap up the little kid two or three times over in it. But, in his own way, this tiny fellow has indicated his aspiration, his desire, to be and to do as his older brother. So David says, 'I will be satisfied when I awake with seeing your form.' Is he implying that the time will come when he too will have a 'Moses experience'? When he will enjoy the same premier intimacy and familiar friendship with Yahweh that none but Moses had previously enjoyed? It doesn't get much better than that. No wonder he can say, 'I will be *satisfied*...with seeing your form.' In verse 14, he said that his adversaries were 'satisfied with sons' but David knows what solid satisfaction is: seeing the face and form of God.

When we come to verse 15 we are standing on holy ground where Jesus' people have often rested their hope. On 14 February 1747, Jerusha Edwards, daughter of Jonathan and Sarah Edwards, died after a week-long fever (cf. Iain H. Murray, *Jonathan Edwards*). She was seventeen. It was no mere sentiment but solid truth that testified to her evident faith and godly life. She had, among other things, devoted herself to nursing David Brainerd, her father's friend, in his last days until he had died four months previously. Her parents buried her next to Brainerd's grave, and Jerusha's gravestone bears the text her parents chose, in the AV (The Authorized Version of the Bible), of course: 'I shall be satisfied, when I awake, with thy likeness.' They knew that's what Jerusha would say if she could. Is that what you can say?

Psalm 18

For the music leader. By the servant of Yahweh, by David, who spoke the words of this song to Yahweh on the day Yahweh delivered him from the grip of all his enemies and from the hand of Saul,

(1) And he said:
I love you, Yahweh, my strength;

(2) Yahweh, my rock and my stronghold and my rescuer;
my God, my rock—I take refuge in him;
my shield and the horn of my salvation, my high fortress.

(3) I call on Yahweh—he ought to be praised,
and I am saved from my enemies.

(4) The cords of death wrapped round me,
and the torrents of destruction terrified me;

(5) the cords of Sheol surrounded me,
the traps of death were right in front of me.

(6) In my distress I call on Yahweh,
and to my God I cry for help;
he hears my voice from his temple,
and my cry for help is before him
    —it comes into his ears.

(7) Then the earth shook and shuddered,
and the foundations of the mountains began to tremble
    —they shook themselves because of his burning anger.

(8) Smoke went up from his nostrils
     and consuming fire from his mouth
          —coals came burning from him.

(9) Then he bent the heavens and came down,
     with thick darkness under his feet.

(10) And he rode on a cherub and flew
     and swept along on the wings of the wind;

(11) he makes darkness his hiding place,
     his covering around him,
     watery darkness, masses of clouds.

(12) Because of the brightness before him
     his clouds passed away
          —hailstones and coals of fire!

(13) Then Yahweh thundered from heaven,
     and the Most High gave forth his voice
          —hailstones and coals of fire!

(14) So he let go his arrows and scattered them,
     and he shot out flashes of lightning and routed them;

(15) then the channels of waters were seen
     and the foundations of the world uncovered,
          because of your rebuke, Yahweh,
          because of the blasting breath of your nostrils!

(16) He sent from on high,
     he took hold of me,
     he drew me out of many waters;

(17) he delivered me from my strong enemy
          and from those who hate me,
     because they were too strong for me.

(18) They confronted me on the day of my calamity,
     when Yahweh proved to be my support.

(19) So he brought me out to a spacious place;
    he rescued me because he delighted in me.

(20) Yahweh treats me in line with my righteousness,
    in line with the purity of my hands he will give back to me,

(21) for I have kept to the ways of Yahweh
    and have not wickedly forsaken my God;

(22) for all his rules are before me,
    and his statutes I will not put away from me.

(23) So I was wholehearted with him,
    and I kept myself from my iniquity.

(24) Yahweh then gave back to me in line with my righteousness,
    in line with the purity of my hands before his eyes.

(25) With the loving you show yourself loving,
    with the wholehearted man you are wholly committed;

(26) with the pure you deal purely,
    but with the perverted you show how convoluted you can be.

(27) For **you** save a suffering people,
    but arrogant looks you will bring down.

(28) For **you** light my lamp,
    Yahweh my God lights up my darkness.

(29) For **by you** I can run against a troop,
    and **by my God** I can leap a wall!

(30) This God—his way is completely right;
    the word of Yahweh has come through fire;
    he is a shield to all taking refuge in him.

(31) For who is God apart from Yahweh?
    And who is a rock except our God?

(32) The God who arms me with strength
    and so made my way completely right,

(33) who makes my feet like those of deer
  and makes me stand upon my high places,

(34) training my hands for war,
  so my arms press down a bow of bronze;

(35) so you have given me your shield of victory,
  and your right hand supports me,
  and your humility makes me great.

(36) You make spacious room for my steps under me,
  and my ankles do not turn.

(37) I will pursue my enemies and overtake them,
  and I will not turn back until they are finished off.

(38) I will shatter them and they will not be able to rise;
  they will fall under my feet.

(39) So you armed me with strength for war;
  you make those who rise up against me bow down beneath me.

(40) And as for my enemies, you have given me their neck;
  and as for those who hate me, I will annihilate them.

(41) They cry for help but there is no savior;
  they cry to Yahweh but he does not answer.

(42) And I will pulverize them like dust before the wind;
  I will empty them out like street mud.

(43) You will rescue me from the hostilities of the people,
  you will place me as head over nations;
  people I have not known will serve me.

(44) As soon as they hear they will obey me;
  foreigners will come cringing to me.

(45) Foreigners will lose heart
  and will come trembling from their strongholds.

(46) Yahweh lives! And blessed be my rock!
    And let the God of my salvation be lifted up!

(47) The God who grants acts of vengeance in my behalf
        and who subdued peoples under me!

(48) He rescues me from my enemies;
    yes, you raise me up higher than those who rise against me;
    you deliver me from the man of violence.

(49) Therefore I will give you thanks among the nations, Yahweh,
    and I will sing praise to your name.

(50) He magnifies the victories of his king
        and acts with faithful love toward his anointed,
        to David and to his seed forever.

6

Surprising Song

Larry Schweikart and Michael Allen pass on an unusual story in their book on American history. One morning in 1816 some folks living in the northeastern United States woke up to a 20-inch snowfall, with some flakes reputed to have measured two inches across. One might stomach all that except that it happened on June 6! Somehow it was connected to something around the world, the eruption of Mount Tambora in Java. Quite a jolt for June anyway.

Now Scripture is sometimes like 1816 in New England. It jolts us, surprises us. I find the Bible regularly throws the unexpected at me. It makes me say things like: 'That's strange'; or, 'I would not have said it like that'; or, 'How absurd that seems to be!' That's partly what makes the Bible so delightful—it persistently runs around my conventions and forces me out of my usual boring ways of thinking. And Psalm 18 is rather typical this way. It is full of surprises. And we may as well approach our study of the psalm that way.

Firstly, then, **we are surprised at such exuberant love for God** (the heading plus vv. 1-3). David simply seems to erupt:

I love you, Yahweh, my strength;
Yahweh, my rock and my stronghold and my rescuer;
my God, my rock—I take refuge in him;
my shield and the horn of my salvation, my high fortress
(vv. 1b-2).

An outburst like that right at the first bowls us over. Why such rapid-fire intensity? Why isn't he more sedate and close-to-the-chest like we are? Why such full-throttle excitement over God?

Here the heading of the psalm helps us, for it tells us this song was David's response to Yahweh's delivering him 'from the grip of all his enemies and from the hand of Saul.' Getting free of Saul takes up 1 Samuel 18–31, almost half of the book of 1 Samuel. Reading those narratives is fascinating—if you're sitting in a library; but for David it was otherwise. He was hated, hunted, and haunted by Saul, pushed from pillar to post, driven to decisions— sometimes disastrous ones—by the desperation of the moment. In one sense it is *painful* reading. Near the end of 1 Samuel, David and his men enjoy the respite of not having to fight with the Philistines against Israel (1 Sam. 29); joyfully they return to their homes in Ziklag—only to find the town burned to the ground and their wives and children pirated by Amalekites (1 Sam. 30). And the thoughtful reader asks, This man is Yahweh's anointed— but when will his sufferings ever cease? Of course, Saul was not his only nemesis—there were foreign enemies

(2 Sam. 8, 10) and more domestic ones (2 Sam. 15–20). But, if you appreciate the background from the heading of the psalm, you may begin to savvy the intensity of its first verses. It's all a bit like that dinner in Simon the Pharisee's house. That woman appears, weeping at Jesus' feet and making a grateful spectacle of her love for Jesus. So he tells Simon a little story of a creditor cancelling the debts of two debtors and follows with the catechism question: Which of them will love him more? Simon is cornered: 'The one, I suppose, to whom he forgave more' (Luke 7:43). Or, à la Psalm 18, the one he delivered more. Too many times, David knows, he was little more than road-kill on life's pavement and Yahweh scraped him up and put him on his feet. And when that happens repeatedly, it infuses love with exuberance.

Note how David addresses and describes Yahweh. The collection of terms speaks of protection, stability, and security. In verse 2, he uses two different words for 'rock,' but they are virtually synonymous. This may hark back to the old witness song of Deuteronomy 32, where 'rock,' we may reverently say, is a nickname for Yahweh (vv. 4, 15, 18, 30-31). One could infer distinct connotations from some of these terms. 'Shield' (2c) is defensive; 'horn of my salvation' may be offensive, if the idea comes from the way an animal might use its horns (note the graphic picture in the later vision in Daniel 8, where the Persian ram and the Greek goat butt their way to conquest); and 'high fortress' (last of verse 2) refers to being placed very high up—out of reach of an enemy's grasp (the same word is used in Psalm 46:7, 11). David heaps up eight or nine 'names' for Yahweh; he does that because he wants to say 'Yahweh has been *all that* to me.'

Perhaps the best way for this point to come home to us is to get a bit pedantic. Put some stress on the conjunctions in the text: 'my rock *and* my stronghold *and* my rescuer' (2a); then 'my shield *and* the horn of my salvation' (2c). What is that little 'and' saying? Isn't it implying that Yahweh always proves to be more than I thought him to be? There is always another 'and' that can be added to the inventory of Yahweh's faithfulness.

In this connection I think of an episode when our sons were young and we were living in Maryland. We lived near a college campus where there was a football field accessible to 'interlopers' when not in official use. Our boys liked to go over to the field because, unlike our yard at home, it had real goalposts and they liked to try their luck/skill at kicking field goals through the uprights. One evening all of us had gone to the field, so Barbara also tried her hand (or foot) in the kicking game. She teed the ball up maybe fifteen or twenty yards from the goalpost, stepped back a bit, then moved up and kicked. Four out of seven of her kicks were good. One sensed that our sons suddenly had a new and tangible respect for their mother. It was a 'wow' moment. After all, here was a forty-year-old woman whom they seemed to know quite well—but she could kick field goals! They had not known that about her. Other kids had mothers, but they were mere mothers. Their mother was a field goal kicker as well.

I think the psalm here follows a similar principle. As David piles up his praise in his description of Yahweh, it's as if he is saying to us: 'Isn't this always the way it is? Yahweh is *so much more* than you at first realize or can express!' Once you grasp his thinking, his unabashed 'I love you, Yahweh, my strength' no longer mystifies you.

Secondly, **we are surprised at such an explosive description of God** (vv. 4-19). Well, it is startling, isn't it, to read of Yahweh's answer to David's prayer and find lines like this:

> Then the earth shook and shuddered...
>
> Smoke went up from his nostrils
> and consuming fire from his mouth...
>
> Then he bent the heavens and came down...
>
> his covering around him,
>   watery darkness, masses of clouds...
>
> the Most High gave forth his voice,
> —hailstones and coals of fire!
>
> So he let go his arrows and scattered them,
> and he shot out flashes of lightning...

What are we to do with a text like this? As we ponder that, someone may come by and whisper the magic word 'theophany' (an appearance of God). The text is depicting Yahweh's intervention in 'theophanic'—and in obviously poetical—language.

How then are we to handle it? Well, taking the heading of the psalm seriously, think of the situation David was in. In 1 Samuel 20:3 he told Jonathan, 'There is but a step between me and death.' That's prose. How does one say that poetically?

> The cords of death wrapped round me,
> and the torrents of destruction terrified me;
> the cords of Sheol surrounded me,
> the traps of death were right in front of me (vv. 4-5).

Quite a bit more dramatic. Now suppose you wanted to say 'God moves the universe to answer His servant's prayer and will unglue creation to rescue him'—how would you do that poetically? You would write something like verses 7-15, nine verses of rapid-fire, mind-expanding, imagination-stretching verse.

Now someone may point out to us that pagan deities could also be described in terms very like verses 7-15. And that is correct. Baal is called 'Rider in the clouds' (cf. v. 10). When Baal gets set to begin the rainy season, 'he will sound his voice in the clouds, flash his lightning to the earth' (cf. vv. 13-14), or we hear that 'Baal sounded his holy voice, Baal thundered from his lips,' which shook earth's high places. Nothing surprising about these similarities. But one also must note the differences. And the difference is that in Yahweh's case the poetry really happened. Look back especially to the book of Exodus: there are the hailstones and fire in the seventh plague (Exod. 9:23-24; Ps. 18:12-13); the figure of the 'blast of the nostrils' brings about the parting of the sea (Exod. 15:8; Ps. 18:8, 15); and then, at Sinai, all the stops are pulled out again—thunder, lightning, cloud, smoke, fire, and Sinai shuddering (Exod. 19:16-20; Ps. 18:7, 9, 11). So David is not simply having a metaphorical fit here; instead he is remembering the exodus God and saying that the exodus God has also come and—in typical form—rescued him.

David himself helps us to interpret verses 7-15, for verses 16-19 seem to be a kind of explanatory footnote to that section. We can put it like this: the *dramatic description* is in verses 7-15, the *calmer interpretation* is in verses 16-19. In the latter, the sound and the fury have abated and

David tells what Yahweh's intervention meant to him. And
he is still using pictures to some extent, not least, it seems,
from Exodus again. Note verse 16:

> He sent from on high,
> he took hold of me,
> he drew me out of many waters.

The verb 'to draw out' (*māšâ*) occurs only here (and the
parallel, 2 Sam. 22:17) and in Exodus 2:10, where either
Moses' natural mother or Pharaoh's daughter says, 'I drew
him out of the water.' It was a wordplay on baby Moses'
name. In the context, the infant's 'drawing out' was his
rescue from Pharaoh's disposal programme for Hebrew
male babies. Here, David beautifully describes Yahweh's
rescue of him: 'he took hold of me, he drew me out of
many waters.' One wonders if he was thinking of Exodus 2
and was essentially saying, 'Yahweh gave me a "Moses
experience."'

All well and good then. But why do we need this rip-
snorting picture of God's intervention? Why didn't David
simply say, 'And Yahweh intervened in a dramatic way' and
have done with it? Much more succinct than spilling all
that ink on verses 7-15. Perhaps a semi-analogy might help.

Some years before I was born, my three oldest brothers
were conscripted (a peril well-known to preachers' kids)
to sing and recite Bible verses at some church function,
perhaps a Christmas programme. I suppose they were
around ages eleven down to five. Many of you have doubtless
witnessed such occasions. Probably you think little of it:
kids are cute, they do well or poorly, and life goes on.
On this occasion, the singing was finished. The oldest boy

recited his Bible verse; number two did the same; number three stood there. Subsequent interrogation elicits the insight that some kind of mental block occurred. Perhaps zealous for the family honor or simply for the opportunity to sit down, number-two boy nudges number-three and whispers, 'Say your verse!' This brought no response. Mute was the word. Probably with more desperation, a bit harder nudge and another hissed 'Say your verse!' At last, a response: number three turned and planted a fist into number two, and I don't recall hearing how the melee ended, except for massive maternal embarrassment. But no one ever forgot it. It sort of stood out in the annals of church children's programmes. In family or congregation, it came up for a graphic re-tell whenever 'Remember when?' time came around. In a word, it was impressive.

I think that's why David takes us through this explosive description of Yahweh. Yes, he could have saved you verses 7-15 and summed it up in one declarative sentence. That would have *expressed* truth but would not have *impressed* you. I propose that David intends to stir your imagination in order to impress you with God. He wants to goad us. He wants to be prickly, for there are dull people who think that God must be as dull as they are—and we sometimes tend to think that way. Our conceptions can become so sluggish and sinful that we begin to think our God is tedious in His ways, anemic in His power, and predictable in His plans. David wants to blow that attitude to smithereens. He wants to show you a God you won't forget.

Then as we come to the third segment **we are surprised by such a blatant claim to righteousness** (vv. 20-29). I imagine more than a few readers recoil a bit when they run into verses 20-24. Perhaps they think it all sounds too crass:

> Yahweh treats me in line with my righteousness...

> for I have kept to the ways of Yahweh
> and have not wickedly departed from my God...

> and his statutes I will not put away from me...

Part of our problem may be cultural or psychological. Some of us have swallowed the idea that the first card one must always play is some variety of false modesty. We may be as self-righteous as they come but it is bad form, we believe, to express it. But, of course, we must not read David's claim through the lens of our twisted misperceptions. What we meet here is similar to what we found in Psalm 17:3-5. Or elsewhere in the Psalms (e.g., 119:30-31, 101-102). These are not boasts of self-righteousness but professions of loyalty and of overall obedience. He is not claiming sinlessness but denying apostasy ('I have not wickedly forsaken my God,' 21b; 'I was wholehearted with him,' 23a); he is not tooting some sort of moral perfection but affirming that he lives under and in obedience to Yahweh's word (v. 22). Because he has walked in obedience to Yahweh's word and has not turned from Him, he praises Yahweh (vv. 25-26) for, in turn, showing faithfulness to him. And if David were speaking in boastful self-promotion, then his next words would be nonsensical ('but arrogant looks you will bring down,' 27b) and he would hardly then go on to indicate that all his sufficiency came from Yahweh (note the emphatic words in vv. 28-29).

I think some Christians are gun-shy of making professions of faithfulness like those in verses 20-24. And

I am tempted to say: Rightly so. For by grace we have become aware that our own hearts are bottomless cesspools of iniquity; our minds and imaginations will ponder any filth; our motives we find are twisted and self-serving; what seem our most laudable designs are often quests for self-deification. There is a certain *misery* in regeneration in that you begin to see the pervasive and pathetic corruption of your own soul. And all this makes me wary of speaking of 'my righteousness' or 'the purity of my hands.'

Which means we likely need Psalm 18! It may bring a proper balance to our perspective. At least it leads us to look more closely at Scripture and, hopefully, be willing to acknowledge and live with a paradox. Look at the matter in a New Testament setting. Remember Paul's assertion before Nero had finished him off: 'I have fought the good fight, I have finished the race, I have kept the faith. Now there is in store for me the crown of righteousness, which the Lord, the righteous Judge, will award to me on that day' (2 Tim. 4:7-8a, NIV). Yet the same Paul had previously said, 'Here is a trustworthy saying that deserves full acceptance: Christ Jesus came into the world to save sinners—of whom I am the worst' (1 Tim. 1:15, NIV). That is Paul the Christian speaking. And he very definitely says, 'I *am* the worst,' not 'I was' or 'used to be.'

Or think of Peter. Remember his stricken outburst after the stupendous catch of fish: 'Go away from me, for I am a sinful man, O Lord' (Luke 5:8). Beside that stab of conviction put Luke 18:28. This text comes after the rich ruler showed he could not 'leave' his wealth, and Peter said, 'See, we have left our homes and followed you.' This was not a boast; it seems simply a matter-of-fact observation,

almost as natural as 'Please pass the butter' at dinner time.
Two statements; both true. I am a sinful man and I have left
all and followed Jesus.

We come back to the Psalms, and we note the angst
over secret faults (19:12), over the hopelessness of guilt
apart from Yahweh's forgiveness (130:3-4), over the folly
of any sort of self-righteousness (143:2). And yet there are
these affirmations of fidelity. We even have a corporate one
in Psalm 44. Not simply an individual, but the body of
God's people protest their loyalty. They are baffled because
they have not enjoyed the blessings promised (Deut. 28:7,
13) but dismal disgrace:

> All this has come upon us,
> yet we have not forgotten you,
> and we have not been false to your covenant.
> Our heart has not turned back,
> so that our steps turned aside from your way.
> But you have crushed us... (Ps. 44:17-19a).

After reading 1 and 2 Kings, it may seem there would be
precious few times when the covenant people could have
said that! But there it is—not a claim to errorless living
but an avowal of walking in basic first-commandment
devotion. Both our sinfulness and our faithfulness may
stand side by side.

This quasi-paradox reminds me of something I read
about an announcement made on an airliner. The pilot came
on the sound system to assure passengers that his particular
airline was 'pleased to announce that we have some of the
best flight attendants in the industry. Unfortunately, none
of them is on this flight.' Obviously a spoof. But, given

that, he was making two affirmations, both—according to him—true, even though it all sounded a bit paradoxical.

And if we are Christians that is where we must stand. On the one hand, we admit how extensive and overwhelming our corruption is; on the other, we contend that by grace we are still holding fast to our Savior. The former should keep us from pride, the latter should save us from despair.

Fourth, we can even say that **we are surprised by such a worldwide kingdom to come** (vv. 30-50). I know some might say they are not surprised because they have read of this coming kingdom throughout the Old Testament. But let's not get ahead of ourselves. Wend your way back to square one. Do you remember when and where David first became king? It was not that long after Israel's disaster on Mount Gilboa, when Saul was removed from the human map. David and his men moved to Hebron, nineteen miles south/southwest of Jebus (Jerusalem). There the men of Judah anointed David king over…well, Judah. That's in 2 Samuel 2:1-4a. At that point, it could be said: Yahweh's chosen king now reigns visibly and actually on earth. But someone might say it almost looks like a hillbilly kingdom. David reigns over but one tribe, in Hebron, in the provincial backwater of Judah. It doesn't look like this will amount to squat. It is clearly the kingdom of God in its mustard-seed form. If you remember this, then verses 30-50 here are more than a bit surprising. It's as if Hebron will, Daniel 2-like, be a stone cut out without hands that becomes a great mountain and fills the whole earth.

I cannot go into the fine details of a very rich passage but will try to give an overall sketch of this 'kingdom' section. And firstly, David describes *what Yahweh has already accomplished* for David in verses 30-36. God's way, he says, has been 'completely right' (v. 30) and he has given David strength (vv. 32, 34), stability (vv. 33, 36), and success (v. 35). Then in verses 37-42 the focus seems to be on *what David will accomplish* by means of Yahweh's help. Admittedly, this point is tied to my translation of these verses. If you compare other English translations, you will find most cast this whole section in 'past' tenses. We don't need an involved discussion on translating Hebrew verbs here. Suffice to say that it is often difficult to know how to translate verbs in the Psalms. In this segment (37-42), I think a number of them are better translated as English futures and that is reflected in my translation. So in the light of how Yahweh has equipped him (vv. 30-36), David anticipates pursuing and finishing off his enemies (37), shattering them (38), annihilating them (40), pulverizing them and, as it were, dumping them out like street mud (42).

Verses 43-45 express *the expansion of the king's reign.* One can't hear tone of voice but David seems a bit amazed as he describes it: 'people I have not known will serve me' (43c); 'foreigners will come cringing to me' (44b); 'foreigners…will come trembling from their strongholds' (45). David's kingship is not simply a pan-Israelite affair but is international in its scope. As David rehearses this, he erupts in his *final praise* to Yahweh (vv. 46-50). Yahweh delivers from 'the man of violence' (48c)—perhaps David refers especially to Saul, who perpetually and perversely lusted after David's death. But David's rescue has extended beyond Saul and his God-given victories include subjugation of foreign peoples (47). Hence David's praise should stretch as far as his kingdom: 'I will give you thanks among the nations, Yahweh' (49).

His praise concludes by confessing that the faithful love that has given David a 'world' kingdom will not be confined to David but will be granted 'to his seed forever' (v. 50c). David understood this when Yahweh first promised him a 'house' or dynasty in what we call the Davidic covenant (2 Sam. 7:1-17). When David responded in prayer to Yahweh's promise, he said: 'and now you extend your promises for your servant's family into the distant future' (2 Sam. 7:19, NJB). We know from reading 1–2 Kings that the kings of David's line (David's 'seed') were often rascals, bums, and apostates. Still, there was a non-negotiable element in Yahweh's covenant to David— Yahweh will somehow establish David's seed and throne forever (Ps. 89:28-29, 36-37), and the time will come when the premier Representative of that seed will have and rule 'the ends of the earth' as His possession (Ps. 2:6-9). So the worldwide kingdom of Psalm 18 eventually brings you to Revelation 11:15.

But we must pay attention to the keynote of David's testimony in verses 30-50. Note where he places the emphasis: not on the saving scope of the kingdom but on the *victorious conquest* of the king in establishing the kingdom. We should say that there are two strands of teaching in the Old Testament (and there is no major tension between them). One you can see, for example, in Isaiah 2:2-3. There peoples and nations are earnestly seeking Yahweh's worship and gladly submitting to Yahweh's word. That is a picture of *conversion* among the nations 'in the latter days.'

But many are not and will not be so wise and docile—they reject, revolt, rebel against the Messiah's kingship and so must be subjugated by force, as one can see in Psalm 2:1-3, 9 (see also Psalm 110). In such passages, the stress is on the necessity of *conquest* in order to establish the kingdom. That is where David places the emphasis in verses 30-50. This makes some folks uneasy; they consider it too 'militant' or 'belligerent.'

Yet one can't simply walk away from this side of the truth. Once B. B. Warfield, one of the 'stars' of old Princeton Seminary's faculty, met the wife of the seminary president on a Princeton street. Mrs. Stevenson was worried about some volatile issues that were soon coming before the General Assembly of the Presbyterian Church. She expressed her anxiety to Warfield: 'Dr. Warfield, I hear there is going to be trouble at the General Assembly. Do let us pray for peace.' Warfield retorted, 'I am praying that if they do not do what is right, there may be a mighty battle.'

Sometimes the 'mighty battle' is the only way. If those who oppose Yahweh's king will not accept His kingship then that kingship must be imposed. If Christ's enemies will not submit to Him then they must be suppressed. We cannot mute this 'conquest' note. Sometimes I think some of our hymns tend to do this. One seems to meet it in the nineteenth-century hymn, 'Lead On, O King Eternal,' in the second stanza:

> For not with swords' loud clashing
>   nor roll of stirring drums—
> with deeds of love and mercy
>   the heavenly kingdom comes.

There is a bit of truth there—and a bunch of error as well. Maybe it's no wonder the church has such an anemic view of the last things. But Psalm 18 seems to testify that the kingdom does not come by peaceful evolution but by successful subjugation. The peace comes after the mighty battle. There is a certain *virility* about the Bible's teaching on this, and for her own confidence the church needs to recover it. Maybe you find such teaching a bit disturbing, but I tried to tell you Psalm 18 is full of surprises.

Psalm 19

For the music leader. A psalm of David.

(1) The heavens keep reciting the glory of God,
     and the skies go on highlighting the work of his hands;

(2) day after day pours out speech,
     and night after night declares knowledge.

(3) There is no speech,
     and there are no words;
     their voice is not heard.

(4) Their line has gone forth throughout all the earth,
     and their words to world's end.
     He has set up a tent in them—for the sun.

(5) And it, like a bridegroom coming out of his bedroom,
     rejoices like a strong fellow to run (his) course.

(6) Its starting-point is at (one) end of the heavens,
     and its circuit all the way to their (other) end;
     and there is nothing hidden from its heat.

(7) The torah of Yahweh is flawless.
          restoring one's life;
     the testimony of Yahweh is reliable,
          wising up the simple.

(8)   The precepts of Yahweh are right,
       making the heart joyful;
   the commandment of Yahweh is pure,
       giving light to the eyes.

(9)   The fear of Yahweh is clean,
       standing forever;
   the rulings of Yahweh are truth,
       they are righteous—every one (of them).

(10) They are to be coveted more than gold,
       even more than much pure gold;
   and they are sweeter than honey,
       and what drips from the honeycomb.

(11) What's more, your servant is warned by them;
       there is great gain in keeping them.

(12) Who can discern (his) errors?
   Clear me of hidden faults.

(13) Hold back your servant also from arrogant sins;
   don't let them rule over me.
   Then I will be without blame,
   and I shall be clear of great rebellion.

(14) May the words of my mouth meet with (your) favor,
   as well as the meditations of my heart in your presence,
       O Yahweh, my rock and my redeemer.

Worship from the Top Down

In his biography of Willie Mays, centerfielder for the San Francisco Giants, James Hirsch tells of the early part of the 1961 baseball season when Mays was off to a slow start. Things were not going very well. And one night it got much worse. The Giants were playing a series in Milwaukee. Late at night, Mays and his roommate, Willie McCovey, went for a walk, purchased some barbecued spare ribs, and took them back to the hotel where they consumed them for a midnight snack. Mays woke up at 3:00 a.m. He vomited, collapsed on the floor, and passed out for a bit. A frightened McCovey called the team doctor, who gave Mays some sleeping pills, which provided only fitful sleep the rest of the night. He arrives at the ball park next day with the stamina of a wet rag. He decides not to play, but while chatting with a teammate near the batting cage he decides to go ahead and take batting practice. He seems to hit pretty well. So he reverses himself and plays anyway.

A strange thing happened. Mays came to bat five times in that game and hit *four* home runs, all of them at least four hundred feet or longer. Only eight other players in the history of the game had ever done that. Who could ever have imagined that that miserable, retching fellow in the hotel room the night before could hit like that the very next day? Most unlikely, and yet clearly true.

I tell you these things because—as so often—baseball is parabolic. You see, there are some scholars who say that we really have two distinct psalms in Psalm 19. Psalm A, we might say, consists of verses 1-6, and Psalm B of verses 7-14. 'A' obviously focuses on the glory of God in creation and 'B' on the character of Yahweh's word; the former dates from an earlier time, the latter is late, say around Ezra's time. Then someone eventually brought them together. But the emphasis and focus of these two 'psalms' is so different, so distinct—so the argument goes—that they could not have constituted one psalm from the first. This is where knowing a bit about baseball helps. For then you know—à la Willie Mays—that a night of vomiting and a day of home runs can easily go together; they are right there, side by side, at the same time. Granted, they are very experientially different and yet can be very temporally compatible. So there is no reason David could not have placed the distinct emphases in this psalm together from the very first.

Now I think Prof. J. L. Mays (no relation to Willie) gives us a very helpful tip for the study of Psalm 19. He suggests we start at the end, with the confession of faith in verse 14: 'O Yahweh, my rock and my redeemer.' Verse 14 then tells us that the 'words' and 'meditation' contained in this psalm compose an act of worship to Yahweh. So David's adoration starts at the 'top,' as he gallivants through the wonders of the visible creation (vv. 1-6), then he 'comes down' to laud the benefits of Yahweh's verbal revelation (vv. 7-10), before expressing the urgent need of his own soul (vv. 11-13). Hence, we have worship from the top down: what we should see (vv. 1-6), what we should hear (vv. 7-10), and what we should say (vv. 11-13). Let us try to unpack the teaching.

First, we meet **what we must see: God's silent splendor** (vv. 1-6). David tells us that the heavens and skies 'keep reciting the glory of God' and 'go on highlighting the work of his hands' (v. 1). The root behind the word for 'glory' has to do with 'weight,' and so used of a person could refer to someone who is 'weighty,' i.e., important and impressive. But 'glory' can also refer to the evidence and outward display that goes with such importance (for a human sample, cf. Gen. 45:13, where English versions may have 'honor'). So the heavens tell us how weighty and impressive God is and the skies speak of 'the work of his hands.' The 'hands' likely implies not only power and ability but care and precision and perhaps intricacy. And this cosmic preaching goes on repeatedly. The verb forms in verse 1 are participles, indicating continuing action (hence 'keep reciting' and 'go on highlighting') and not one-shot or occasional activity. Verse 2 reinforces the point, especially with its first verb, 'pours out,' associated with the idea of bubbling up or out. Allan Harman nicely catches the implication: 'creation cannot contain itself, but constantly proclaims the glory of God' (*Psalms*, Christian Focus, 1:202). The heavens and skies are simply bursting to tell us of their Maker and keep pumping out their testimony about Him.

Strange thing about this stellar proclamation though—
it is totally silent (v. 3). Actually, the way verses 3-4b
'explain' this plops us down in a sharp paradox. On the
one hand, we find no speech, no words, and, really, no
voice (v. 3). No sooner do we read that than verse 4 tells
us, 'Their line has gone forth throughout all the earth,
and their words to world's end.' One can justify various
translations for the first line of verse 4, e.g., 'their voice'
or 'their call,' though I have kept the traditional 'their line.'
In this option the line is a measuring line that scopes out
an allotted portion. The idea is that all the earth is the
'territory' assigned to the heavens and skies in which to
bear their witness. But however we take the first line,
the next line of verse 4, 'their words [have gone forth] to
world's end,' fly in the face of verse 3. Verse 3 says there
are no words, verse 4 says there are! A paradox, a seeming
contradiction. One gets the idea that the psalmist is trying
to make us think. And here it helps to remember that some
contradictions do not really contradict.

I remember reading one of Paul Boller's stories about a tiff
on the floor of the U. S. Senate. Alexander Stephens (who
would become Vice-President of the Confederate States)
apparently railed, 'My opponent is not fit to carry swill to
swine.' There were cries for order and a demand for Stephens
to apologize, which he did, by meekly saying, 'I do apologize.
The Senator is absolutely fit for the duty to which I referred!'
One statement is a denial, the other an affirmation—and yet
they both make essentially the same point.

So we need not be troubled when the psalm says there
are no words and then seems to say there are. The buzzwords
now for this are 'non-verbal communication'—mute

communication that still communicates. It's the sort of thing that happens when we are invited to someone's place for dinner. All the eating may be over, the conversation has gone on around the table for some time. Then I may feel the pressure of my wife's foot against mine or—another under-the-table ploy—the tap of her fingers on my leg. Nothing is said. Yet what she is 'saying' is, 'It's time we were going; you need to say something to that effect.'

David seems to give us a *sample* of this mute testimony in what he says of the sun (vv. 4c-6). Note how playfully he puts it: the sun enjoys the skies as a God-given tent (v. 4c). Then he speaks of the sun's daily 'run' across the skies (as an earth-located observer would view it; vv. 5-6b). If a Hebrew were a Scot, he might say the sun is God's wee lad who, like a bonnie bridegroom, makes his trek across the sky without being much puggled at the end of it. But it's important to realize that you couldn't have fun with the sun like that if you were a pagan. In paganism, the sun was worshiped. In Egypt, it was represented by the god Re; in Mesopotamia, the sun was viewed as Shamash, the guarantor of justice. But none of that here. The sun is de-deified—it is simply God's daily cosmic courier. In the Bible, the sun is relieved of the crushing burden of deity—maybe that's why there seems to be a bit of bounce and frolic in verses 5-6!

The psalm then is saying that the work of creation lets you see the silent splendor of God. True, you need to know more than the 'work of his hands' will tell you. But this silent witness does proclaim truth to you—and does so with a certain mirth that you will never find in the pathetic melancholy of paganism.

And we know that not all God's 'silent splendor' is—as in the psalm—astronomical. Some of it lies much closer to hand. George Marsden tells of young Jonathan Edwards' fascination with spiders. By close observation of 'forest' spiders, he discovered how they could seem to fly. The filament they released from their tails was lighter than air, so by letting enough of it out they could go up or simply float in the air. They could float in light breezes by either letting out or contracting the lengthy filament on which they rode, and he was sure they did it with 'a great deal of their sort of pleasure.' From this the teenager inferred: 'We hence see the exuberant goodness of the Creator, who hath not only provided for all the necessities, but also for the pleasure and recreation of all sorts of creatures, and even the insects and those that are most despicable' (*Jonathan Edwards: A Life*, 65).

Daily work for the sun and pleasure for spiders—this and far more, but all very quiet. But that's no reason you should be blind to it, or fail to stop and worship.

Secondly, the psalm sets before us **what we must hear: God's clearest speech** (vv. 7-10). 'There are no words' when God speaks in creation (vv. 1-6), but there *are* words when he speaks in Scripture (vv. 7-10). Notice also the sudden and repeated use of the name Yahweh in these verses, as if to clue us that we have to do not only with the cosmic God 'at a distance' (vv. 1-6) but the covenant God who is near, Yahweh, the God who is present among His people (Exod. 3:12-15). The text implies that He has drawn near to us in His Word.

In verses 7-9, David describes the *character* of Yahweh's word. And I think the best way to grasp his intent is simply to wade through each statement he makes. First, he says, 'The torah of Yahweh is flawless, restoring one's life.' I have simply retained the Hebrew term torah. It is often translated 'law' in English versions. But torah is broader than law; it refers to doctrine, teaching, instruction. This instruction is 'flawless.' Bible readers often meet the Hebrew adjective behind this translation in the requirements for sacrificial animals—'without defect' or 'without blemish' (e.g., Lev. 1:3). Or one might think of the root idea involved— to be whole, complete. One might say Yahweh's torah is 'all there,' that is, has and offers everything you need. In any case, flawless. And it restores one's life. The idiom is the same as Psalm 23:3. The idea is not that of spiritual conversion but of reviving and invigorating one who has been exhausted perhaps by trouble or calamity.

We are also assured that Yahweh's testimony 'is reliable, wising up the simple' (v. 7b). The 'testimony' sometimes refers to what was written on the tablets Moses brought down from Mount Sinai, the ten commandments (Exod. 31:18; 32:15; 34:29). Some expositors hold that the word-root carries an undertone of warning. This would be exactly what the 'simple' one needs. One who is simple is naïve, inexperienced, and therefore all too open to, and oblivious of, danger (cf. Prov. 1:4; 14:15). So the warning of Yahweh's commandments is just what he needs—they 'wise him up.' Think of the child who has never learned to ride a bicycle. Some parents remember installing 'training wheels' on the back wheel of a bike. These give a certain stability to the two-wheeler until a kid gets the skill to ride without them. In the meantime, they keep that kid from falling off and making a mess of himself. Don't press the analogy, for we never outgrow the need for Yahweh's 'testimony.' But the point here is that the warnings of

Yahweh's law put in place certain safeguards that keep us from ruin.

'Precepts' (v. 8a) may carry a distinctive note of authority. Its root points to 'what is appointed,' i.e., appointed by Yahweh, and therefore meant to be kept (Ps. 119:4). But if 'precepts' breathes authority and sovereignty and dogmatism (!), they are nevertheless 'right' and they keep 'making the heart joyful.' This is oxymoronish to the world. To those outside the covenant, the corollary of sovereignty is drudgery, but to covenant insiders the corollary of sovereignty is delight. That what Yahweh imposes should incite joy in His people utterly mystifies Wormwood and all his disciples in this age.

In the last of verse 8, David refers to 'the commandment of Yahweh.' Note the singular. He does not refer to the various commands and demands in particular but to the sum, to the whole body of what Yahweh requires of His people. All that 'commandment,' he assures us, is 'pure,' that is (as Allen Ross points out), without any imperfection or pollution. And it has the specific effect of 'giving light to the eyes.' This is sometimes understood as giving needed guidance or direction. But the clause may point in a different direction. In 1 Samuel 14, King Saul had gone on oath, forbidding any Israelite troops to taste food—they must get on with pursuing Philistines. Sometimes royalty and stupidity are combined, and this was one of those times. Knocking off Philistines takes energy and it's hard to have that with no snacks. But Saul's son, Jonathan, didn't know anything about his father's prohibition—he was, after all, already fighting Philistines when Saul held his press conference and made his pronouncement. So in the pursuit the troops entered a forest, where they saw honey for the taking. However, they didn't, because of Saul's oath. But Jonathan, not knowing any better, grabbed some. To the troops' protests, Jonathan said, 'See how my eyes have brightened because I have tasted a bit of this honey' (1 Sam. 14:29; I alluded to this under Psalm 13). He means he has had a fresh burst of energy. That may be the idea behind Yahweh's commandment 'giving light to the eyes.' Yahweh's word refreshes and energizes and renews the strength of His weary people. How often they have found it to be so!

In verse 9, the pattern changes: 'the fear of Yahweh is clean, standing forever.' Instead of some synonym for Yahweh's word, we hear of the attitude and disposition that word produces in one's life, and that fear—that trembling, trusting reverence—is 'clean.' 'Clean' is a term from what we sometimes call the ceremonial law (cf. Lev. 10:10-11) and here it refers, as Allen Ross says, to what is acceptable in the presence of God because it is not in any way polluted or perverted. And this fear goes on 'standing forever'; it never goes out of date or out of style in God's eyes. Then in the last of verse 9 David mentions the 'rulings of Yahweh' and affirms they are 'truth.' One could say that 'rulings' are particular applications of principles. In Exodus 20:1-17, Yahweh lays down the ten words or commandments for Israel. Then in Exodus 21–23 He sketches samples of how these commandments are to be applied in various circumstances of Israel's life. These are his 'rulings' (Exod. 21:1). So not only the torah or the commandment considered as a whole is flawless and pure, but even the particular details of Yahweh's word are truth; indeed, every one of them is 'righteous.'

Now that we've looked at these individual statements about Yahweh's word in verses 7-9, we need to say that

David is not so interested in our analyzing such statements! What I mean is that David is not trying to get you to distinguish 'testimony' from 'precepts' or 'commandment' from 'rulings.' Rather, he wants to build up for you a *total picture* of Yahweh's true, reliable, soul-renewing, life-preserving, joy-inducing, energy-giving word that will hit you like a ton of bricks and make you say something like verse 10. David moves from describing the character of God's word (vv. 7-9) to expressing the *desirability* of God's word (v. 10). He doesn't just want you to see what Yahweh's word is like; he wants you to say, 'I must have it.'

How desirable is Yahweh's word? David speaks in terms of its value ('to be coveted more than gold') and its enjoyment ('sweeter than honey'). But note the verb he uses: 'they [the various forms of God's word] are to be *coveted* more than gold.' Most of our versions clean it up to read 'desired.' And that is okay. But it doesn't hurt to remember that this verb (*ḥāmad*) often carries a negative coloring. It is the verb of the tenth commandment, 'You shall not covet' (Exod. 20:17). It describes the tree Eve contemplated as 'covetable for the wisdom it could give' (Gen. 3:6, cf. NJB). It is the verb Achan uses in confessing why he squirreled away plunder he saw in Jericho (Josh. 7:21). But the Psalm implies there is a *holy* coveting you should have; there is a *pure* lust that ought to consume you, namely, to possess Yahweh's written word in all its truth and benefits.

Which is always the response of God's servants when they are at their best. And William Tyndale was. The man who had given England a Bible in its own tongue had taken refuge in Antwerp. He was betrayed by a false friend and handed over to the tender mercies of 'the church' for eventual execution. For some time he was kept in prison in Vilvoorde, a little north of Brussels, where he braced himself to endure the winter months. S. M. Houghton tells us that a nineteenth-century researcher discovered a letter of Tyndale's in Belgian archives, a letter written to the governor of the prison. It reads in part:

> I entreat your lordship, and that by the Lord Jesus, that if I am to remain here during the winter, you will request the Procureur to be kind enough to send me from my goods which he has in his possession, a warmer cap, for I suffer extremely from cold in the head.... A warmer coat also, for that which I have is very thin: also a piece of cloth to patch my leggings.... I wish also his permission to have a lamp in the evening, for it is wearisome to sit alone in the dark. But above all, I entreat and beseech your clemency to be urgent with the Procureur that he may kindly permit me to have my Hebrew Bible.... (*Sketches from Church History*, 121-2).

Some pathos in that: a warmer cap, a warmer coat, a lamp at night, but, *above all*, my Hebrew Bible. They strangled and burned him (1536) but that sacred avarice for God's word remained to the last. Nor is this some special attitude that only revered Bible translators have. If the God who has quietly spoken His cosmic word (vv. 1-6) has stooped to speak clearly in the pronouns, participles, adverbs, and verbs of His torah (vv. 7-9), surely I should meet such godly grammar with an answering obsession, surely His excellent word (vv. 7-9) must be met by my unrelenting appetite (v. 10).

Thirdly, David tells us **what we should say**, as he gives us a glimpse of **God's prayerful servant** (vv. 11-14).

In verse 11, we meet with the first personal reference in the psalm—'your servant.' And as Yahweh's servant he speaks—we could say—both negatively and positively regarding Yahweh's commandment, testimony, precepts, etc. On the one hand, he is 'warned' by them; on the other, there is great reward in keeping them. Then he launches into a marvelous prayer (vv. 12-13), and I want you to take note of the concern or the *anxiety* of his prayer.

He is worried over undetected errors and hidden faults: 'Who can discern (his) errors? Clear me of hidden faults' (v. 12). Sin may be present but we may not identify or perceive it. When David speaks of 'hidden faults,' he does not mean they are hidden from other people but from himself. There are wrongs that we simply have not detected; they have not come up on our conscious radar. I am simply not sharp enough to see and expose all my guilt. Once realize this and you won't be plagued by the fantasy of perfectionism. The truth is you have no idea how sinful you are.

He is also anxious over willful sins: 'Hold back your servant also from arrogant sins' (v. 13a). Here David speaks of sins committed in pride and insolence. He wants pardon from secret sins (see v. 12), and he wants *preservation* from deliberate sins (here), for he knows their enslaving power ('don't let them rule over me,' 13b); he prays this way because he knows he is prone even to deliberate, willful, eyes-wide-open sins.

And, finally, David mentions 'great rebellion.' Note the way he puts it: 'Then I will be without blame, and I shall be clear of great rebellion.' That 'then' is a crucial connector. He is saying that if Yahweh clears him of hidden faults and holds him back from arrogant sins, then he will not come to the point of committing 'great rebellion.' What does he mean by that? I think he refers to the next step up—or, should we say down?—from the 'arrogant sins' of 13a. In other words, apostasy, falling away from and totally renouncing Yahweh as his Lord. So we find a pattern that moves from hidden faults (12) to arrogant sins (13a) to decisive apostasy (13b). The idea seems to be that this last is a genuine danger, that there can be a path from errors to insolence to apostasy, and earnest prayer is called for in the face of each instance and possibility.

Christians may err here. Some may think that since they have the assurances of Jesus (e.g., John 10:27-28) or of the apostles (e.g., 1 Peter 1:3-5) no Christian need be worried about the specter of apostasy. But the Bible never wants us to use its assurances to avoid its warnings. More commonly perhaps, Christians simply settle with a self-reliant attitude that so much as assumes, 'Oh, I could never do *that*.'

Such cocky security always reminds me of the only time I can recall my mother laughing uncontrollably. I was a lad and was with my father and mother in a mid-western state, attending a Bible conference. We stayed on this occasion in a local motel. This was before the days of card keys; the key to the motel room was a normal key on a ring, along with an oblong piece of green plastic with the motel logo and address on it. One morning my father could not find the key to our motel room. He looked in his trousers and checked every spot in the room he could think of. Finally, my mother suggested that perhaps, when we had come in the previous night, he had simply left it in the outside lock of the door. One never forgets momentous pronouncements and his—as he walked toward the

door—was: 'Oh, I wouldn't do that; that would be dumb!'
Having said so, he opened the door and extracted the key.
It took Mom a long time to recover.

So don't think you are somehow immune to 'great
rebellion.' Don't tell yourself something really stupid like,
'Well, David was an Old Testament believer and didn't have
the clearer assurance that I have and so worried himself
unnecessarily about apostasy.' That is not the Bible way.
For if the believer does not commit apostasy it is precisely
because he fears it and cries out to God to save him from
it. It is alarm over apostasy that God uses to keep you from
it (cf. Heb. 3:12), and if you think it cannot touch you, if
you suppose that you are somehow above it, you are already
on your way to it. The place of true safety is to be God's
prayerful servant and make verses 12-13 your own prayer,
or maybe pray the third stanza of Robert Robinson's hymn:

> O to grace how great a debtor
>   daily I'm constrained to be;
> let that grace now, like a fetter,
>   bind my wand'ring heart to Thee.
> Prone to wander—Lord, I feel it
>   —prone to leave the God I love:
> here's my heart, O take and seal it,
>   seal it for Thy courts above.

Could we say that God's glory is most truly glorious not
when it displays itself in the vast expanse of space but in
the servant in his/her closet, praying in response to the
scrutiny of God's word? Is there a contrast here between
the sun (vv. 4b-6) and the servant (vv. 11-14): the one
runs across the skies to the glory of his Creator, the other
falls on his knees crying to his redeemer?

Psalm 20

For the music leader. A psalm of David.

(1)   May Yahweh answer you in the day of distress;
      may the name of the God of Jacob set you up high;

(2)   may he send help to you from the sanctuary,
      and give you support from Zion.

(3)   May he remember all your offerings,
      and may he accept your whole burnt offering. Selah.

(4)   May he give you what your heart desires,
      and may he fulfill all your plans.

(5)   We will shout for joy over your victory,
      and in the name of our God we will fly our banners.
      May Yahweh fulfill all you ask of him.

(6)   Now I know that Yahweh has saved his anointed;
      he will answer him from his holy heaven
      with mighty saving deeds, done by his right hand.

(7)   Some ... in chariots,
      some ... in horses,
      but we, we will implore the name of Yahweh our God!

(8)   They are subservient and have fallen,
      but we, we have taken our stand and are held up.

(9)   O Yahweh, save!
      The king will answer us in the day when we call.

8

ROYAL ATTENTION

Royalty holds an attraction even for, perhaps especially
for, non-royal people. I don't know the gamut of opinion
in the U.K. about the royal family, but in my country
anything notable about them (and I don't mean mere
gossip) attracts huge attention. We were in Australia when
William and Kate were married, and my wife made
sure she was in front of the TV for the whole spectacle.
I can still remember the fascination I felt reading about
a young Queen Elizabeth II in my 'Weekly Reader' paper
in elementary school! For some reason, presidents and
secretaries of state don't pack the 'pizazz' of queens and
princes. And so those of us who don't have royalty seem to
eat it up vicariously.

Psalm 20 reflects a people transfixed on royalty, only
the royalty is their own. They are focused on the fortunes
of David their king as he prepares to lead Israel's forces
to war. Their attention and concern are justified, for, as it

goes with the king and the troops, so it goes for the people. Their fortunes are locked up with the king's. Think of the angst involved: the king goes off to fight, say, in Syria (cf. 2 Sam. 8) long before cell phones and satellites or even Morse's telegraph—and a people must wait anxiously for the arrival of human messengers. So, as another 'campaign season' arrives, the people pray for the king (vv. 1-5) and the king confesses his and his people's faith (vv. 6-8).

Before we dive into the psalm, notice its vocabulary and pattern. The key verb 'answer' wraps the psalm in verses 1 and 9 (and also appears in verse 6); verse 1 also speaks of the 'day of distress,' while verse 9 places against that the 'day when we call.' There are three references to the 'name' of God (vv. 1, 5, 7) and four references to the root for 'save'/'salvation' (vv. 5 [where I translated 'victory'], 6 ['saved' and 'saving'], and 9). The psalm is carefully and artfully constructed.

There is some debate over who is 'speaking' in various segments. Verses 1-5 are most easily taken as the prayer of the people (or someone speaking for the people) for the king as he goes off to war. It seems reasonable to take verse 6 as the king's own words. Verses 7-8 (note the 'we') could be the people's response—or these verses could simply continue the king's speech from verse 6, with the king including the people's confidence with his own. I tend to the latter and take all of verses 6-8 as from the king. Verse 9 is then a tailpiece that sums up both previous sections of the psalm.

One more 'intro' matter. Since the psalm seems to be about the king, you may be disappointed. You may think there is a 'distance' here, as if the psalm has nothing to do with you. It is not as 'immediate' for you as Psalms 13 or 17. But have patience. It's sort of like driving up to the intersection nearest your house and seeing municipal trucks sitting there and an excavator digging out a trench and amassing a huge pile of unsightly dirt. You think little of it, for you think it has nothing to do with you. But six days later you revise your thinking as the trucks and excavator are on the street edge of your front lawn with their trench and dirt. They are installing a new gas line down your road. The mess at the intersection had more to do with you than you imagined. And I suspect you will find the same with Psalm 20—but only if we start digging into it.

First, in verses 1-5 you discover **the prayer we can still pray.** And let's take some time to survey the details of this prayer before dealing with its significance and application for us.

The people pray Yahweh will answer the king 'in the day of distress' or trouble (v. 1a). Conceivably, this could mean the king is facing the necessity of a defensive war rather than an offensive one. The 'distress' may mean that the nation's borders have come under attack, though we simply can't be sure about this. What is especially fascinating in verse 1 is the combination of 'answer,' 'day of distress,' and 'God of Jacob.' Speaking of Yahweh as the 'God of Jacob' means that He is the covenant God who makes commitments and sticks to them (cf. Gen. 28:13-15). But this particular vocabulary 'pool' necessarily conjures up Jacob's words to his clan in Genesis 35:3. In a fresh situation of danger, he spoke to his clan of going back to Bethel and making an altar to 'the God who answers me in the day of my distress and has been with me wherever I have gone' (ESV). What a testimony that is. What a God to have in life's dark hours!

By selecting this background, the psalm may be saying, 'We have a Jacob God for a David situation.' And they pray this God of Jacob will 'set the king up high.' We met this word-root, 'to set up high,' in Psalm 18:2 as a noun, which I translated as 'my high fortress.' The idea is that God sets his servant in a high place out of and above the reach of his enemies or would-be destroyers.

In verse 2, the people ask Yahweh to send help and support to the king 'from the sanctuary' and 'from Zion.' In verse 6, the king is confident that Yahweh will answer him 'from his holy heaven.' There is no conflict here. Yahweh's throne is 'in the heavens' (Ps. 11:4)—that is the ultimate source of His help; but Yahweh's earthly sanctuary is 'the place of [his] feet' (Isa. 60:13) and is, we might say, the mediate channel of His help. It was the appointed place of Yahweh's presence where His people might expect His aid (see the expectation throughout Solomon's prayer in 1 Kings 8:29ff.). Calvin sets the two side by side: 'Thus, under the visible sanctuary, which was made with hands, there is set forth the fatherly goodness of God, and his familiarity with his people; while, under the heavenly sanctuary, there is shown his infinite power, dominion, and majesty.'

In verse 3, the people mention the king's burnt offering and accompanying gift offerings. They are not alluding to some legalistic ritual. Rather, the king has used the God-provided means of atonement (for the burnt offering as an atoning sacrifice, see, e.g., Lev. 1:4), and in light of that they pray that Yahweh will give him his heart's desires (4a), fulfill his plans and strategies (4b), and all his requests as well (5c), and they themselves vow to delight in and celebrate the victory Yahweh gives him (5ab).

Once more let us remind ourselves of the reason for this fixation on the king's success. The welfare of the people rested on the success of the king. Disaster for the king spelt the same for the people. There is a somewhat amusing analogy to this 'one and many' situation in the War between the States. Charles Dana was an observer at the Battle of Chickamauga. He was at staff headquarters behind Union lines. He had been taking a nap when he heard the most infernal racket of musketry and cannon. The Confederates had overrun a Union flank and were pouring in. Dana says that the first thing he saw as he sat up was General Rosecrans, a devout Roman Catholic, crossing himself. Dana knew instinctively that if the *general* was crossing himself, the army was in deep trouble. He jumped on his horse and vamoosed (Benson Bobrick, *Master of War*).

That is the thinking here. In fact, we know from 2 Samuel 21:17 that a time came when David's troops would no longer allow David to go to war with them. David had had a close call in combat, so his men prevented his going into battle with them anymore: 'You will never again go out with us to battle, and you must never put out the lamp of Israel.' David was the 'lamp of Israel.' Were his life snuffed out in battle, Israel would flounder in darkness and confusion. His death would spell disaster for them. In one sense, David *is* Israel. It is this sort of thinking that lies behind calling Israel's king 'our shield' (Ps. 84:9). The people are intricately united to their king.

Do Christ's people still pray this way in A.D. time? We pray something like this and yet differently, for David's son and David's Lord already sits enthroned (Ps. 110:1). Unlike

David, Christ is not going out to fight the Philistines or Syrians or to open up a new 'campaign season.' Rather, the Root of David 'has won the victory' (Rev. 5:5), and, in the wake of His cross-work, He has risen, ascended, and sits at God's right hand 'in the heavenly realms, far above all rule and authority and power and lordship and every name that is named, not only in this age but in the coming one' (Eph. 1:20-21). He has already won the war, has vanquished every invisible and visible foe—only the 'clean up' work remains. So, unlike the prayers in Psalm 20, we do not pray for Jesus to be victorious; we pray because He *has been* victorious. That has altered everything.

Leon Morris (in his *Expository Reflections on the Gospel of John*) tells of contralto Marian Anderson. Toscanini had told her she had the voice of the century. She was a sensation throughout Europe; she once gave a concert at the White House for the Roosevelts and the king and queen of England. One Easter Day she sang beneath the Lincoln Memorial to a crowd of over 75,000. So when a reporter once asked her what was the greatest moment of her life, she had a plethora to choose from. Her choice? 'The day I went home and told my mother she needn't take in washing anymore.' That was the day that changed everything. And once the day came when Jesus began to reign, our prayers have changed a bit. We still celebrate His victory (cf. v. 5), but we do not pray for it. We pray He would manifest, display, make open and public His victory, that He would impose it on those who flatter themselves that they can resist it, that He would indeed allow His people to see the days of the Son of Man (cf. Luke 17:22). We pray, but on the basis of a victory already achieved.

But there is another way we can still pray Psalm 20. I am thinking especially of verses 1-2, and I suggest that we may legitimately hijack this prayer for the King's people. As we noted, though the prayer was originally for the king specifically, the fortunes of the people were intricately tied up with the king's—and so why may not verses 1-2 also be prayed for the king's subjects? Books written on biblical interpretation tend to spawn their own buzzwords and terminology, so there's no reason we can't come up with some of our own. So in this case we might appeal to 'trans-situationism': the dilemma of the king also involves the people and so the prayer can be rightly offered for them as well. (You might try dropping 'trans-situationism' as you drink coffee with two or three after church—see if you get a blank look or a knowing nod!) Actually, Psalm 20:1-2 is my favorite benediction to use for the Lord's people at the close of worship, simply because it is so very applicable to so many of them. How many of them standing there are on that day of worship also in a 'day of distress,' or, as the standard version has it, 'day of trouble.' How desperate some of them are for 'help' from the sanctuary and 'support' from Zion.

We may sometimes lose sight of the multiple, hidden troubles of the people of God. I was recently impressed with this when reading of William Cunningham, premier nineteenth-century theologian of the Free Church of Scotland. I have read some of his lectures and have known of him for years, though I was aware of few details about his personal circumstances. Then I read an 1852 letter he had written to Dr. Hodge, of Princeton Seminary. Cunningham told how he and a colleague had spent a month on the Continent, going as far as Strasbourg and Paris. But when he returned, he found his youngest child, a girl eighteen months old, already dead, though not buried, and another child, a boy of six years, dying. The latter lived five more days after Cunningham's return. How the 'day of trouble' dogs the lives of God's servants—it is simply all too typical.

What more appropriate benediction could there be for the congregation I served? I stand at the end of the service, look them in the eyes as I scan their faces, and announce Yahweh's blessing. But what faces do I see? A man living with nearly constant physical pain; a young wife whose husband has decided to walk out on her; an older man who now comes alone because his wife got what she wanted from him and left; wives who have recently become widows; children in a tailspin of depression; a father on the edge of financial disaster. It is their day of trouble. What a delight to speak Psalm 20:1-2 to this body. And yet a bit hard, for often the words would catch in my throat as I looked at them and said:

> The LORD answer you in the day of trouble,
> the name of the God of Jacob protect you;
> may he send you help from the sanctuary,
> and give you support from Zion.

Yet what better 'blessing' could they have?

Now, secondly, in verses 6-8 we find **the position we must still take**. Here I assume the king is speaking.

And the king seems completely confident of Yahweh's help: 'Now I know that Yahweh has saved his anointed' (v. 6a). That may sound a tad premature since the king has not yet gone out to battle. But the verb really is what Anglos would call a past tense. He is so convinced of Yahweh's saving him that he depicts it as having already occurred. It's like Paul's verb 'glorified' in Romans 8:30. It hasn't happened yet; it's still future; but since God has determined to do it, it is so certain that it can be spoken of as already having occurred. Look at verse 6 here again. I wonder if David's Descendant, Jesus, sometimes pondered Psalm 20:6 as He braced Himself for the ordeal of His cross. Might its confidence have galvanized His own soul as He lay down His life for us?

David's ringing certainty is the same in verse 8, as he pictures his opponents as already defeated. Yet this infectious confidence rests on whether God's king and people have assumed the right position—and that is spelled out in verse 7. Here is the stance we are called to take.

Verse 7 is actually a little choppier than it appears in some of our translations. The verb doesn't occur until the end of the verse. I have retained the roughness: 'Some… in chariots, some…in horses, but we, we will implore the name of Yahweh our God!' The verb 'implore' is literally, 'cause to remember,' but this 'remember' verb often seems connected to verbal worship. As Alec Motyer says, we 'bring the Lord to remembrance' by invoking His name. That is the sense it has, for example, in 1 Chronicles 16:4, where the Levites were 'to invoke [literally, 'cause to remember'], to thank, and to praise' Yahweh. Hence here in the psalm, 'implore' is a proper rendering. But, of course, if we implore the name (which stands for all that Yahweh is and has declared Himself to be) of Yahweh, it means we are calling upon Him, leaning upon Him, trusting Him—in this case, to the exclusion of horses and chariots. If you 'remember' Yahweh, you will take a non-horse, non-chariot position!

But what made horses and chariots so all-fired desirable? In David's time, chariots seemed to be pulled by two horses and manned by a two-man crew. They served as mobile firing platforms and sometimes could be used in the shock tactic of a frontal charge. One writer tells us that in Egypt the king's chariot was considered a divine being and praises were sung to the various chariot parts. Horses and chariots were the 'fighting edge' of human power, and the danger was that too often a substitution occurred and God's people would trust in such human armaments rather than in Yahweh's arm (cf. Isa. 31:1-3). Yahweh's people must not lean on mere human power, even power with steroids like horses and chariots.

The problem with mere human resources is that too much can happen to them. Chariots are a case in point. In Joshua 11 (vv. 6-9) a northern coalition was poised to fight Israel, but Joshua struck them in a surprise attack and decimated their chariots before they had the opportunity to reach suitable ground where they could assemble them and use them effectively. Putting together the bits of Judges 4–5, it seems a rainstorm mucked up the Plain of Esdraelon and Sisera's vaunted chariots became bogged down helplessly.

It can be the same story even when nations graduate to tanks and planes and missiles and drones. It's not that the Americans didn't have planes at Pearl Harbor in 1941; it's just that they were disarmed and parked in bunches (to prevent sabotage), so that Japanese pilots came into Hickam and Wheeler Fields and decimated them. It's not that the Germans didn't have plenty of tanks as they attacked the U.S.S.R. in the same year. But the 'season of mud' began and soon temperatures plummeted. Fuel would freeze and, at 31 degrees (F) below zero, German tanks were next to useless. It's not that the Arab allies joined against Israel lacked planes. But by the end of the day on June 5, 1967, the Israeli Air Force had destroyed nearly the entire Egyptian and Jordanian air forces—and half of Syria's—before they ever got off the ground.

I am not saying that nations should not have military material for their defense; I am only illustrating the fact that the flaunted resources of human power can be very fragile and flimsy. And the people of God, at any rate, are charged not to place their trust there. They must take a different position. We must shun our favorite props and our most cherished substitutes and keep running into the tower of Yahweh's name. Our whole lives seem to be experiments in learning *not* to trust our artificial supports. Again and again we have to learn that only the nail-scarred hands of the resurrected Jesus are adequate to hold us up.

Now we come to verse 9. You will note that it reads differently from a number of English versions. Not: 'Yahweh, save the king!' and so on. But: 'Yahweh, save! **The king** will answer us in the day when we call.' The traditional Hebrew text divides the verse this way, and I think it is likely correct to do so. So, as we come to the end of the psalm, verse 9a ('Yahweh, save!') sums up verses 1-5, while verse 9b gathers up the confidence expressed in verses 6-8. And translating the verse this way makes 'the king' in 9b the emphatic subject of the clause and also indicates that in this case the king is not David but Yahweh, the true king. And isn't this, after all, our deepest assurance?

One of my wife's hobbies is quilting. Lap quilting, I think they call it. She plans and pieces her quilts, some small, some king-size, then uses her hoop and begins quilting—investing hours, while traveling or watching a football game on TV, or while conversing with family or friends. And she has not escaped some good-natured mockery for her quilting mania. Sometimes in our travels we might stop somewhere for lunch; the boys would pile out, we would walk toward the restaurant, and I would hear, 'Did you lock the car? I don't want anyone stealing my quilt.' It all seemed a bit ludicrous. Not that there couldn't be quilt thieves stalking the parking lots of our nation. To hear Barbara talk, you would have thought that quilts were the hottest stuff on the market. But looked at through her eyes, her paranoia made excellent sense. She had designed and assembled that piece of art, had laboriously quilted stitch after single stitch, had invested hours upon hours of work in that project—and there was no way she would leave it unprotected. That's the confidence that oozes out of verse 9b. At the end of the day we know that '*the* king,' Yahweh, will answer us. And we know that because the kingdom is His and these people are His, and because He has so invested Himself in the success of His kingdom and the welfare of His people—that He simply refuses to allow any foe to flush them down the sewer-line of history.

Psalm 21

For the music leader. A psalm of David.

(1) Yahweh, in your strength the king finds gladness,
and in your deliverance how greatly he rejoices!

(2) You have given him the desire of his heart,
and you have not held back the request of his lips. Selah.

(3) For you come to meet him with wonderful blessings;
you place a gold crown on his head.

(4) Life was what he asked from you
—you gave it to him,
length of days forever and ever.

(5) How great is his glory because of your deliverance;
splendor and majesty you confer upon him.

(6) For you make him (the medium of) eternal blessings;
you cheer him with gladness with your presence.

(7) For the king trusts in Yahweh;
and because of the faithful love of the Most High
he will never be shaken.

(8) Your hand will find all your enemies,
your right hand will find out those who hate you.

(9) You will make them like an oven on fire
           at the time of your appearing;
         Yahweh, in his anger, will swallow them up,
           and fire will consume them.

(10) You will cause their fruit to perish from the earth,
         and their seed from the sons of men;

(11) for they intended evil against you
         —they planned a scheme;
         they will not succeed.

(12) For you will make them (turn their) backs;
         with your bow-strings you will aim at their faces.

(13) Rise up, Yahweh, in your strength!
         We will sing and raise psalms about your might.

9 Looking Both Ways

When I began visiting in the United Kingdom and walking the streets of its cities, I became very grateful for vigilant friends who looked out for me. Our two nations drive on different sides of the road. And so, whether I was crossing a street in London or Leicester, in Inverness or Glasgow, my instinct was to look for traffic coming in a U.S. direction—in which case I could easily get smeared by traffic coming in a U.K. direction! Fortunately, friends protected me from such error. But sometimes one has to negotiate the convolutions of such urban traffic all alone. In which case I sometimes found help by looking down at the pavement at an intersection; there I sometimes found the words painted, 'Look this way,' with an arrow pointing in the proper direction. I was grateful. It was almost as if those words were saying, 'We've had Americans at this intersection before who didn't know what they were doing, and so here's a tip to help you.' But alas, not all intersections have such avant-garde lettering, and so I simply adopted the policy of looking both ways, no matter what.

Now that is what Psalm 21 does. It looks backward to Psalm 20, where the Lord's people had prayed for the king's success and preservation in war. So the first part of Psalm 21 looks back and gives thanks for answered prayer (vv. 1-6). Then verses 8-13 look forward and anticipate the complete triumph of the kingdom of God in the future. You note that our psalm both begins and ends by speaking of 'your [=Yahweh's] strength' (vv. 1, 13). That strength delivered the king in the recent past (Pss. 20; 21:1-6); and the people look to that same strength to consummate the kingdom of God in the future (vv. 8-13). In between these two sections, verse 7 may stand somewhat by itself; but, for the most part, Psalm 21 is a psalm that looks both ways, both backward and forward. I think the teaching of the psalm will most easily come out simply through making several observations.

First, we notice that God's people are **remembering a particular deliverance** (vv. 1-6). As noted, the memory of this psalm goes back to its 'partner,' Psalm 20, where the Lord's people had prayed for the safety and victory of the king as he prepared to go to war. And now they declare that Yahweh has indeed answered both their petition and the king's: 'You have given him the desire of his heart, and you have not held back the request of his lips' (v. 2). Hence we are dealing here with the fodder for thanksgiving. Yahweh has given a positive answer to Israel's prayers and their gratitude seeps through the cracks of this psalm.

But there's more. In verses 3-6, it's as if the people open up the whole matter again and expand on what was involved in Yahweh's answer to their prayers. So verses 1-2 furnish their basic recognition of Yahweh's goodness; note that the verbs in verse 2 are 'past' tenses—this has already taken place. But the verbs change in verses 3-6. Let me avoid technicalities and simply say that it seems best to translate them as present tenses in English. But it seems that in these verses the people flesh out what they simply mentioned in summary in verses 1-2.

And so…they highlight the *recognition* Yahweh lavished on the king, the gold crown for his head (v. 3b) and the glory and splendor he conferred on the king in his victory (v. 5). Naturally, they emphasize the *preservation* of the king: 'life was what he asked from you—you gave it to him' (v. 4). He came through the perils and combat of war unscathed. And yet Yahweh gave him far more than that, for He granted him 'length of days forever and ever' (v. 4b). This may refer to the ongoing royal line of David that Yahweh decreed would go on 'forever' (2 Sam. 7:16; Ps. 89:3-4). And that would link up with the blessing of *covenant* in verse 6a. Granted, this verse is a bit difficult but the idea seems to be that the king is the source or means (I have supplied 'medium') of benefits to God's people. In 2 Samuel 7, the original 'Davidic covenant' passage, Yahweh had already indicated that through David's kingship he would provide stability and security for Israel (2 Sam. 7:10-11a). All the gifts and goodness Yahweh heaps upon the appointed head of His people overflow to that people as well. But perhaps the king's supreme good is the sheer *joy* he has because of Yahweh's very presence (v. 6b). Whether rehearsing

Yahweh's answer to their primary request (vv. 1-2) or the plethora of bounties bestowed along with that answer, the people of God are careful to remember the particular deliverance their king—and they—have received.

Is that not enough for us to take away from this first section of Psalm 21—that we remember particular deliverances with particular thanks? Too often we are not particularly particular about particularizing. We tend to be masters of the grand (and rather meaningless) generalization. 'We thank you for your many, many blessings,' we ramble along in what we call prayer. Really? Can we take the time to name one or two? To dwell upon them in praise? There's a delightful expression in the Westminster Confession of Faith, in its chapter on repentance unto life, where it says, 'It is every man's duty to endeavor to repent of his particular sins particularly.' The same principle should control our praise.

This matter often reminds me of those times as a lad when I was privileged to hear my mother's prayers. Occasionally my father was away from home overnight and Mom would then lead family worship. She would read Scripture, then we knelt to pray. Her petitions were longer and more precise than my father's. I always knew what was coming. She would mention each of her five sons by name and pray for each in some detail as she thought appropriate for that boy. By this time most of them had flown the nest and only I, as the 'caboose' of the family, was left. But each son was prayed for in order and specific petitions offered for him in line with, I think, both my mother's suspicions as well as the desires of her heart! There was always something deeply moving about this. Of course, these were primarily petitions, but I think the same specificity should mark our praise. That may be why Joshua 12 is as long as it is. Instead of short-circuiting and saying that Joshua and Israel struck down over thirty kings west of the Jordan, the writer lists all thirty-one of them by name, as if itemizing all thirty-one flavours of the faithfulness of God. Isaac Watts got it right:

> O bless the Lord, my soul,
> nor let his mercies lie
> forgotten in unthankfulness,
> and without praises die.

Secondly, in verse 7 we find the king **enjoying an indestructible stability**: 'for the king trusts in Yahweh; and because of the faithful love of the Most High he will never be shaken.' Most English translations have '*through* the faithful love of the Most High,' but the Hebrew preposition can have a causal force and I have translated it that way: '*because of* the faithful love....'

What kind of assurance is this verse giving to David, the believing king? 'Faithful love' translates the word *hesed* (English versions translate it variously: e.g., steadfast love, lovingkindness, etc.). [*h*]*esed* was at the heart of the covenant Yahweh had cut with David in 2 Samuel 7. There Yahweh had promised David an ongoing dynasty, an eternal throne (v. 16). But it might be that any one of David's descendants would not have David-like faith or walk in David-like obedience; we know from Judah's history that some Davidic kings were rascals and rogues. That's why there was a 'disciplinary clause' or a 'judgment rider' in the Davidic covenant (2 Sam. 7:14b). 'But,'

Yahweh assured David, 'my *ḥesed* I will never take away from him [David's seed] as I took it away from Saul' (v. 15). In spite of human sinfulness and historical hazards there is a defiant indestructibility about Yahweh's covenant with David. It has to do with his *ḥesed*, his faithful love—it will never fade, falter, or fall (cf. Ps. 89:27-37). We know this proved to be the case. For after Israel's kingless years in exile and the bleak days after they returned to the land, it may have seemed Yahweh's covenant had bitten the dust and His kingdom had gone underground at best. But then a shoot popped up from the stump of Jesse (Isa. 11:1) and a Nazareth virgin heard the decree about her son:

> He will be great and will be called the Son of the Most High. And the Lord God will give to him the throne of his father David,
> and he will reign over the house of Jacob forever, and of his kingdom there will be no end (Luke 1:32-33, ESV).

Yahweh's *ḥesed* had carried the day! There was no way He would allow His David-plan to be stashed away on the historical shelf. That is the confidence David has in this psalm: he knew there was no way Yahweh would allow His David-scheme to fall to the ground.

But is such a bulwark of assurance only for covenant kings like David to enjoy? Or is it for Doug and Debbie Israelite as well? Certainly, the latter. Remember Psalm 103? It describes those who fear Yahweh as both forgiven (vv. 6-12) and frail (vv. 13-16). Then, in verse 17, David pits Yahweh's *ḥesed*-love against that frailty. No doubt about it: our life is flimsy stuff—it really can have that here today-gone tomorrow shape to it (vv. 15-16). 'But the *hesed*-love of Yahweh is from everlasting to everlasting upon those who fear him, and his righteousness to children's children' (v. 17). The everlasting-formula brings to mind Psalm 90:2, where Moses speaks of the eternity of God: 'from everlasting to everlasting you are God.' And now Psalm 103:17 says that Yahweh's *hesed* is as eternal as Yahweh himself. So my fragile life, which is always, as we say, 'day to day,' is taken up, wrapped around, and held fast in an everlasting love. The text begs you to draw the conclusion: Yahweh's *hesed*-love then will keep hold of you through death, into resurrection, and beyond. And so 'he will never be shaken' (Ps. 21:7) describes my lot as much as it does David's.

Rowland Hill (d. 1833) has left us a hymn based on Psalm 55:22. One of the stanzas goes like this:

> He sustains you by His hand,
> He enables you to stand;
> *those whom Jesus once has loved*
> *from his grace are never moved* [emphasis mine].

That is why we also will 'never be shaken.' Jesus' *hesed* is love that refuses to budge, that won't let go. Jesus' *hesed-love* is not simply love—it is love with super-glue on it.

Finally, in verses 8-13, we see God's people **anticipating a final triumph**. The people are still the ones speaking, or, perhaps more likely, one representing the people, who speaks about the king. The 'future' tenses in verses 8-12 point to the ongoing success of the king. David's most recent victory is not his last victory but is part of a continuing pattern which will culminate in the decisive and final triumph of his kingdom, a triumph that takes place when David's Descendant appears in glory and puts down all his and his people's enemies (2 Thess. 1:6-10).

Now notice the *form* this triumph takes: the elimination of the king's enemies. The speaker underscores the *certainty* of it: 'Your hand will find all your enemies, your right hand will find out those who hate you' (v. 8); the *totality* of it: 'You will make them like an oven on fire,' 'Yahweh... will swallow them up, and fire will consume them' (v. 9); indeed, they will be eradicated root and branch (v. 10); and the *justice* of it—they are only getting their just deserts, for they plotted, schemed, and connived to overthrow the regime of Yahweh's appointed king (vv. 11-12). I suppose you could call this teaching the 'dark side' of the kingdom; but you must realize that if you pray for God's kingdom to come you are by that very petition praying that all that opposes and assaults God's kingdom will be put down. The Heidelberg Catechism makes this clear (No. 113); it says that part of what we are praying when we pray 'Thy kingdom come' is:

Destroy the devil's work;
destroy every force which revolts against you
and every conspiracy against your word.

The victory of the kingdom means—requires—the defeat of its enemies. This understanding ought to infect our thinking, praying, and living, but too often it gets lost in either our apathy or our sentimentality.

I like the story about Alexander Pope, Scottish pastor in the 1700s (told by Donald Beaton, in *Some Noted Ministers of the Northern Highlands*). He served at Reay, where the local inn seemed to draw a larger crowd than the church.

One Lord's Day evening after church service, Mr. Pope was sitting outside the manse, which was very near the inn. A couple of inebriates invited Pope to join them. He refused and rebuked them sharply for desecrating the Lord's Day. They were miffed, went into the tavern, and returned in a few minutes with a crowd of intoxicated associates. Pope rose from his seat, keeping his back to the wall. Did I mention that he usually carried with him a small, stout club, called 'the bailie'? The leader of the thugs decided to make a seeming gesture of 'peace' and filled a glass with whiskey, offering it to Pope. The pastor refused and apparently rebuked the mob again. They were in no mood for sermons; the bottle was hurled at the minister's head and the leader rushed at him. A quick and nicely aimed blow with the club dropped the fellow at the pastor's feet. Several more tried to attack and met a similar fate. The sight of several brutes splattered on the ground, groaning in agony and pain, restored enough sobriety to dissipate the crowd. It was all quite simple. If Mr. Pope was to stay on his feet, they must be knocked off theirs; if he was to remain in one piece, some skulls had to be cracked. If it sounds brutal, the principle is clear: if the kingdom comes, opposition crumbles; if the kingdom triumphs, all that despises and opposes and assails it must be taken out.

Recognizing this conflict element can direct our prayers as we await the kingdom in final form. Jesus commands us to love our enemies, and one way we are to do so is to pray *for* those who persecute us (Matt. 5:44). When, however, the enemies are not only our enemies but God's enemies, there are times when we also pray *against* persecutors. In 1964, in what used to be the Belgian Congo, communist rebels, the Simbas, were committing atrocities, not least against the church and her missionaries. These rebels imposed themselves in the Sunday services of the African Inland Church in Bunia. One of them stood up and began extolling his leaders. After the people had endured this, the pastor asked Miss Fitenia Papalaskalis to lead in prayer. She was the daughter of a Greek man and a Congolese woman and, as a mulatto, would be particularly despised by the rebels. Still, she stood and prayed in front of these gun-toting Simbas:

> Lord, we ask You to help us in our hour of great need. You know that Congo is in need of You at this time. You know that we have evil men who have come into our area recently. Many of them are thieves and murderers. They beat and kill our people for no reason. Lord, judge these evil men. Bring your wrath down on these terrible men. Put the fear of God into them. Save us from these people and bring us peace and freedom once more we pray. In Jesus' name. Amen.

She sat down. The Christians looked on her with awe, the Simbas looked and remained silent. The pastor preached. When he gave the benediction, the Simbas left quietly (see James and Marti Hefley, *By Their Blood*, 533-4).

That was a gutsy prayer—yet one driven by the assumption that if God's kingdom is to come then those bludgeoning His people must be neutralized. It is a proper way to pray: anticipating Christ's final victory, we plead for him to give us anticipations of that victory even now in the thick of the church's sufferings. With David and his congregation we join our voices in crying, 'Rise up, Yahweh, in your strength!' (v. 13a).

Psalm 22

For the music leader. 'The doe of the dawn.' A psalm of David.

(1) My God, my God, why have you forsaken me?
Why are you far from saving me,
(from) the words of my roaring?

(2) My God, I call by day and you do not answer,
and by night as well I am not silent.

(3) But you are holy,
enthroned on the praises of Israel.

(4) In **you** our fathers trusted,
they trusted, and you granted them escape.

(5) To **you** they cried out and were delivered;
in **you** they trusted and were not disappointed.

(6) But **I** am a worm and not a man,
the scorn of men and despised by the people.

(7) All who see me deride me,
they let go with their mouths,
they shake (their) heads.

(8) 'Commit (yourself) to Yahweh!
Let him provide escape for him;
let him deliver him,
since he delights in him.'

(9) But you are the one who pulled me from the womb,
the one who made me trust on my mother's breasts;

(10) upon **you** I have been thrown from birth;
     from my mother's womb you are my God.

(11) Do not be far from me,
     for distress is near,
     indeed, there is no one to help.

(12) Many bulls have surrounded me,
     strong bulls of Bashan have closed round me.

(13) They have opened their mouths against me,
        a lion tearing and roaring;

(14) I am poured out like water,
     and all my bones are out of joint;
     my heart has become like wax,
     it melts within me;

(15) my strength has dried up like a potsherd,
     and my tongue is stuck to my jaws,
     and you place me in the dust of death!

(16) Yes, dogs have surrounded me,
        a congregation of evildoers has closed in on me,
        they have pierced my hands and my feet.

(17) I can tell all my bones;
     they gawk, they look at me;

(18) they parcel out my garments among them,
     and over my clothing they cast lots.

(19) But **you**, Yahweh, do not be far off!
     O my strength, rush to my help!

(20) Deliver my life from the sword,
     my prized possession from the power of the dog;

(21) save me from the mouth of the lion,
     and from the horns of the wild ox—you have answered me!

(22) I will tell of your name to my brothers,
   in the midst of the assembly I will praise you.

(23) Fearers of Yahweh, praise him!
   All the seed of Jacob, honor him!
   And stand in dread of him, all the seed of Israel!

(24) For he has not despised
   and he has not detested
      the affliction of the afflicted,
   nor has he hidden his face from him,
   but when he cried to him, he heard.

(25) You are the source of my praise in the vast assembly;
   I will pay my vows in the presence of those who fear him.

(26) Let the poor eat and be satisfied;
   let those who seek him praise Yahweh;
   may your hearts live forever!

(27) Let all the ends of the earth remember
      and turn to Yahweh,
   and let all the clans of the nations worship before you,

(28) for kingship belongs to Yahweh,
   and he rules over the nations.

(29) All the prosperous ones of the earth shall eat and worship,
   all those who go down to the dust will bow down before him
      —even the one who cannot keep his life alive.

(30) A seed will serve him;
   it will be told about the Lord to the coming generation.

(31) Let them come and tell of his righteousness
      to a people yet to be born—
   that he has accomplished (it).

10

THE ANSWER OF THE FORSAKING GOD

In 1917, Cecil B. DeMille produced *Joan the Woman*, his
first epic, and took the film to New York for the censors to
approve. After the screening, a clergyman who was in the
group said he found nothing offensive in the picture. But
a woman on the censor board disagreed. There was one
thing that had to be deleted. 'It's the line,' she said, 'where
Joan says, "My God, my God, why hast Thou forsaken me?"'
DeMille asked her if she knew who had first spoken the
line. The woman stonewalled; that made no difference, she
claimed. 'It means that God would forsake someone, and it
has to come out' (Boller and Davis, in *Hollywood Anecdotes*).
Well, it didn't. And we can also be thankful that the fine
folks who assembled the Psalms did not edit it out either.
Psalm 22 stands here in all its head-scratching mystery and
bare-knuckles severity. It didn't have 'to come out.'

The psalm breaks down into two major divisions and
the words of verse 21c ('You have answered me!') are

the hinge between the two segments. First, we look at verses 1-21, which we may call **the terror of God-forsakenness**.

Note what the psalm tells us about the shape of forsakenness. What does it look like? Well, here it consists of *silence*, divine silence (vv. 1-2). 'Why are you far... (from) the words of my roaring? My God, I call by day and you do not answer' (1b, 2a). Nothing panics the servant of God like the silence of God (see Pss. 28:1-2; 109:1ff.). Yahweh is the God who hears prayer (Ps. 65:2). What are we to think when He doesn't?

But forsakenness comes also in the form of *scorn* (vv. 6-8), the scorn of men who mock and ridicule one even for his faith. Verse 8 seems to quote these mockers. Apparently this jeering comes from folks who are, at least in name, part of the covenant people, for they use 'Yahweh,' the covenant name of God. In the first line of verse 8 they are either telling the sufferer to commit himself or else to commit his matters and circumstances to Yahweh. In any case, it is all in sarcasm. It's as if they are throwing Psalm 37:5 with razors all over it in his face. The upshot of the rest of verse 8 is that God will not mess with delivering anyone like him.

The scorn of men (vv. 6-8) seems to aggravate the silence of God (vv. 1-2), but now this forsakenness reaches its most appalling form in the total *subjugation* of this afflicted man to his enemies (vv. 12-18). This is the most detailed and extensive of these three 'forsakenness' segments.

He describes his suffering in 'beastly' terms. Bulls surround him (v. 12), but in the next verse bulls become a lion that tears up its prey and roars. In verse 16, dogs circle round—these are not the house-pet variety but the half-wild, garbage-moochers of the Near East. But the canines are human: they are a 'congregation of evildoers' (v. 16b). The 'beast' imagery implies, as Alec Motyer says, that the assault lacks any of the constraints of humanity. Indeed, the ordeal is too much: he is enervated (v. 14), exhausted (v. 15), and emaciated (v. 17a).

The assault is fatal. 'They have pierced my hands and my feet' (v. 16c). That translation has been debated. You may have a footnote in your Bible indicating that the traditional Hebrew text reads, 'like a lion my hands and my feet.' 'Like a lion' translates one Hebrew form. But if the last letter of that form is slightly extended it becomes a verb, 'they have pierced.' In 1997, a Hebrew text from Nahal Hever was published which actually reads 'they have pierced'—and this Hebrew text is a thousand years earlier than our traditional Hebrew text (C. R. Gren, in *Journal of the Evangelical Theological Society*, 48 [2005]: 283-99). The Greek translation (Septuagint) from about 200 B.C. also took it this way. I think then that we have good grounds for translating 'they have pierced.' And then verse 18 only reinforces the extremity of his suffering, for if his enemies have his garments and clothing *then he is totally within their power and they can do with him whatever they will.*

We must pause before this 'subjugation' section (vv. 12-18) because it raises the conundrum of this psalm. If the psalm comes from David (see the heading), it yet goes beyond David. Clearly, as Yahweh's anointed David was hated, hunted, and hammered. First Samuel 18 and following relate his almost unrelieved sufferings. There were times when the 'dogs' nearly got him (see the end of 1 Samuel 23). But he never faced anything so final or total as described here in Psalm 22.

What to make of this? I think we must distinguish between Davids! There is clearly the *historical David* who speaks in this psalm and doubtless describes much of his own suffering. But David was a man and king in covenant with Yahweh (2 Sam. 7); Yahweh had promised to establish David's royal line in an everlasting kingdom (cf. Ps. 89:1-4, 19-37). One could say David knew there would be a super-David to come. So I suggest David also speaks here as the *dynastic David*, as the covenant representative who can depict his coming Descendant in terms of his own suffering, and yet a suffering that goes beyond the bounds of what David himself had endured. In this sense, we could say he speaks as a prophet (cf. Acts 2:30). David spoke *out of* his suffering and yet *beyond* his suffering and *into* the suffering of Another.

But we have more to see; we must see not only the forms forsakenness takes but also how the suffering one walks by faith in such God-forsakenness. The structure of verses 1-21 is very important here. Note how the silence (vv. 1-2), scorn (vv. 6-8), and subjugation (vv. 12-18) sections are each followed by an affirmation of faith or plea for deliverance—and these latter segments each begin by focusing emphatically on Yahweh Himself: 'But you…' (vv. 3, 9, 19). Each description of his misery is met by the memory of faith or the desperation of petition. He first appeals to *history* (vv. 3-5). He confesses that the forsaking God is nevertheless the holy God, even the God in whom 'our fathers' trusted. The second person pronouns in verses 4-5 are emphatic: 'in *you* our fathers trusted,' 'to *you* they cried out,' 'in *you* they trusted.' Yahweh proved to be their delivering and non-disappointing God. In his period of divine forsakenness (vv. 1-2), the psalmist stills remembers that he belongs to a people who have celebrated a history of divine faithfulness.

Then, in verses 9-11, he appeals to *experience*, what he claims has been true in his own past. It's fascinating to link verses 9-11 to his despair in verse 6. There he had complained, 'But I am a worm and not a man.' Yet in verses 9-11 he so much as says, 'But I am a very special kind of worm!' It was as if Yahweh was the midwife or doctor who delivered him at birth (9a) and cared for him there. If Yahweh was so preoccupied with him at the very beginning (vv. 9-10), is he likely to go on hiding His face from him?

Finally, we could say his last appeal is one of *emergency* (vv. 19-21). As someone has said, verses 12-18 describe nothing less than an execution—hence the sheer desperation: 'Do not be far off...rush to my help' (v. 19). And, strangely, it is when the power of the dog, the mouth of the lion, and the horns of the wild ox (vv. 20b-21) have done their worst that Yahweh answers him (21c).

What then are we to make of this terror of God-forsakenness? We have already noted that some of this suffering (especially vv. 12-18) is so extreme that it goes beyond the historical David and depicts the agonies of the 'David' who was to come, our Lord Jesus Christ. But it originates in the anguish of David's own believing experience—which implies that it could be the lot of any of the saints. Some Christians might dispute this. They might say that Old Testament believers may have suffered this sense of God-forsakenness but New Testament believers, living on this side of the cross and empty tomb, have far greater assurance and are not afflicted with such agony (which would make the Psalms mostly useless to Christians). Such folks would hold that God—at least now—never withdraws the radiance of His face nor allows those who fear Him to walk in darkness without any light. A regimen of reading good Christian biography would soon cure this naïve view. In the meantime, however, Charles Spurgeon might keep us straight. He once said:

> I believe it is a shallow experience that makes people always confident of what they are, and where they are, for there are times of terrible trouble, that make even the most confident child of God hardly know whether he is on his head or on his heels (C. H. Spurgeon, *Autobiography*, Banner of Truth, 1:103).

We may not care for such candor but it may save us from terrible disillusionment later. Some time ago I was discussing a malady I had had with my doctor. It had cleared up subsequently but I was inquiring how prevalent my problem was. He told me it was 'not common, but not unusual.' That may be the best way for Christians to look at this matter of divine 'abandonment'—not common (mercifully) but not unusual (so not surprising). J. C. Ryle has put it well:

> No doubt there is a sense in which our Lord's feeling of being 'forsaken' was peculiar to Himself, since He was suffering for our sins and not for His own. But still after making this allowance, there remains the great fact that Jesus was for a time 'forsaken of the Father', and yet for

all that was the Father's 'Beloved Son'. As it was with the Great Head of the Church, so it may be in a modified sense with His members. They too, though chosen and beloved of the Father, may sometimes feel God's face turned away from them. They too, sometimes from illness of body, sometimes from peculiar affliction, sometimes from carelessness of walk, sometimes from God's sovereign will to draw them nearer to Himself, may be constrained to cry, 'My God, my God, why hast thou forsaken me?' (*Expository Thoughts on the Gospels*, on Mark 15:34).

This may be of immense help whenever we find ourselves walking in darkness and still clinging to the God who doesn't seem to be there.

Secondly, let us turn to **the testimony of deliverance** in verses 22-31. However, before we hear the testimony we had better locate the deliverance. It's in the last line of verse 21: 'from the horns of the wild ox—you have answered me!' Being at the mercy of a wild ox and tossed on its horns is about as far from deliverance as one might imagine. And yet exactly at that point we hear this staccato exclamation, 'You have answered me!' It is the hinge of the psalm, the transition from terror to testimony.

Granted, verse 21c seems terribly abrupt, but still some of our English versions do not handle it so well. The NIV takes the verb as an imperative and as a part of the petition ('save me'); the ESV is better but translates interpretively, 'you have rescued me.' But the verb (literally, to answer) was deliberately chosen because it forms the antithesis to the use of the same verb in verse 2. There he said, 'You do not answer,' but here, here, is the reverse: 'You have answered me!' The ESV muddies this intended play on the verb.

To appreciate this deliverance we must remember the appalling hopelessness from which it appears. I have always liked William Sangster's story about *The Flixton*. It was a small Hull steamer and one day in 1918 it was making its way up the English Channel. The look-out man noticed a white line coming swiftly toward the ship. No doubt about it; it was a torpedo from a German submarine which was, right at that moment, rising to the surface to view the deadly damage of its work. The look-out naturally gave a shout and everyone on board ran to that side of the ship. But it was hopeless; nothing could save them. It was too late to turn the ship, and all knew that in a few seconds they would be blown to bits. Then, Sangster says, an amazing thing happened. Only a few yards from its target, something went wrong with the mechanism of the torpedo. It reared its nose out of the water, turned course, and shot straight and fast on the very path it had just traversed. Before those hapless British seamen knew what had happened, they saw the torpedo smash into the German sub and blow it immediately to the bottom. That is how verse 21c ('You have answered me!') should strike us coming from verses 12-21b—it is impossible relief out of hopeless despair. And clearly that was the pattern of the gospel events: in face of the darkness of Golgotha there shines an empty tomb and an occupied throne (cf. Acts 2:32-35). The resurrection and ascension are God's answer to the forsaken Messiah. (And many of Messiah's people can attest a similar pattern in their own exit from darkness to light.)

And so in verses 22-31 the Delivered One declares his praise 'in the midst of the assembly.' This testimony breaks down into two sections: he has a word for the 'brothers'

(22), that is, the congregation of believers (vv. 22-26) and then a word for the world (vv. 27-31; note 'the ends of the earth' in v. 27).

Look at his testimony to his 'brothers' in verses 22-26. By the way, I am aware of the use of this text in Hebrews 2:11-12, but right now I want you to grab hold of these verses in the setting of the psalm. I won't cover every detail of these verses, but what you must see is the *reason* for Messiah's praise and also the reason why his people (v. 23) should praise Yahweh; note the explanatory 'For' at the start of verse 24:

> For he has not despised
> and he has not detested
> > the affliction of the afflicted,
> nor has he hidden his face from him,
> but when he cried to him, he heard.

Have we ever thought that our condition is so gross, so unlovely, so repulsive that God could not stand to touch it? Have we perhaps imagined that he might well despise both the affliction and the afflicted? Is this text then not a balm in Gilead when we are walking in thick darkness and heavy trouble? And if God is hiding his face from us, don't we gain solace from the end of the verse? If Messiah was not finally cast off in his most extreme distress, is it likely we will be in any of our lesser troubles? If he at last knew God's smile, can't we expect to see the same once more? So the Delivered One passes on this testimony to you: 'He has not despised and he has not detested the affliction of the afflicted'—and you can carry that text into the pit with you.

The second half of the sufferer's testimony is a word for the world (vv. 27-31). The verbs in verse 27 can be translated as though making a statement or as implying a call. I think the latter is preferable:

> Let all the ends of the earth remember and turn to Yahweh,
> and let all the clans of the nations worship before you,
> for kingship belongs to Yahweh,
> and he rules over the nations (vv. 27-28).

All is headed toward worldwide homage—what else?, implies verse 28. Is this to be seen as the outcome of sufferings endured in verses 1-21? Likely so; in any case, Psalm 86:9 sums up all of verses 27-31: 'All the nations you have made will come and worship before you.'

Verse 29 of our psalm is difficult but seems only to reinforce the previous point. A good number of expositors take the 'prosperous ones' and 'those who go down to the dust' as pointing to both ends of a spectrum, the hearty, healthy, and well-heeled and the dying and destitute. These and all those in between will worship and bow down. So when verse 30 declares, 'A seed will serve him,' we can grasp who the 'seed' is. According to the context, it includes the 'seed of Jacob' and 'seed of Israel' who fear Yahweh (v. 23) and also 'the clans of the nations' who will worship and bow before Him (vv. 27-29). 'A seed'—a Jewish-Gentile worldwide seed—'will serve him.' 'Is God the God of Jews only? Is he not the God of Gentiles also? Yes, of Gentiles also' (Rom. 3:29, ESV). This piece of testimony ought to foster both a deep satisfaction over its certainty and an aching longing for its complete fulfillment.

Perhaps children can be our teachers here and show us the attitude we ought to have. Archibald Alexander Hodge and Mary Elizabeth Hodge were the two oldest children of Charles and Sarah Hodge. (I have already mentioned Charles in previous pages; he was a rightly revered professor of 'old Princeton' Seminary.) When these children were ten and eight years old respectively, they gave a letter on 23 June 1833 to Mr. James Eckard. Mr. Eckard was a Princeton Seminary graduate soon on his way to Ceylon for missionary labors there. The letter was given to Eckard but was addressed to 'the heathen.' Here is the letter:

> Dear Heathen: The Lord Jesus Christ hath promised that the time shall come when all the ends of the earth shall be His kingdom. And God is not a man that He should lie nor the son of man that He should repent. And if this was promised by a Being who cannot lie, why do you not help it to come sooner by reading the Bible, and attending to the words of your teachers, and loving God, and, renouncing your idols, take Christianity into your temples? And soon there will be not a Nation, no, not a space of ground as large as a footstep, that will want a missionary. My sister and myself have, by small self-denials, procured two dollars which are enclosed in this letter to buy tracts and Bibles to teach you. Archibald Alexander Hodge and Mary Eliz. Hodge, Friends of the Heathen (David B. Calhoun, *Princeton Seminary*, 2 vols. [Banner of Truth], 1:193).

Isn't that marvelous? Of course, you can wrinkle up your nose and complain that it 'sounds like a bit of nineteenth-century overly optimistic eschatology.' Maybe so—but you would be foolish to do so. For this avid longing for the complete gathering of a worldwide people is the response Psalm 22 is trying to drag out of you.

The last verse (31) implies that there will be an ongoing testimony about Yahweh 'that he has accomplished (it).' The text is abrupt. The Hebrew provides no object for the verb (to accomplish, or, simply, to do). We almost have to supply 'it.' But what then is that 'it' that Yahweh will have accomplished? Is it the redemption of His people through the finished work of the Forsaken One?

Psalm 23

A Psalm of David.

(1)   Yahweh is my shepherd;
      I will never lack anything.

(2)   He makes me lie down in grassy pastures,
      he guides me beside restful waters;

(3)   he restores my life;
      he leads me in paths of righteousness
            on account of his name.

(4)   Even though I walk through the valley of the
            shadow of death,
            I will not fear disaster;
      for you are with me;
      your club and your staff—they comfort me.

(5)   You prepare a table before me,
            right in front of my enemies;
      you have anointed my head with fragrant oil;
      my cup simply runs over.

(6)   Only goodness and faithful love will pursue me
            all the days of my life,
      and I shall turn in to the house of Yahweh
            for length of days.

11

SHEPHERD GEOGRAPHY

I want to treat Psalm 23 under the rubric of 'shepherd geography,' but first we must meet the Shepherd. Verse 1 strikes three keynotes in regard to the shepherd. The first is *intimacy:* 'Yahweh is my shepherd.' In Exodus 3:12-15, God indicated to Moses that 'Yahweh' was theological shorthand for 'I will be present is what I will be'; an expanded paraphrase might be, 'I will be present with my people to be whatever they need me to be for them.' Most of our English Bibles translate this divine name as 'the Lord' (in small caps), and, when they do so, we know that the covenant name of God (Yahweh) stands behind it. Now I am not about to overthrow centuries of tradition; but you need to see that we lose something with the translation 'the Lord,' for the simple reason that 'the Lord' is a title, not a name, and conveys more distance than intimacy. One may sometimes be around a group of (perhaps older) men and hear one of them refer to his wife. 'The wife doesn't eat Brussels sprouts,' or 'the wife went shopping for shoes,' or 'the wife asked me to vacuum the carpet for her.' One can talk like that and folks know to whom such a fellow is referring. But he is using a title and it seems a bit cold and detached. 'The wife' this, 'the wife' that. Maybe he even addresses her as 'Wife.' One can do that; it works. But I never call my wife 'the wife'; I call her Barbara, because that's her name. And here David calls God by His 'first' name, Yahweh. It is not only calling Him '*my* shepherd' that connotes intimacy but the very use of God's covenant name.

Then there is a note of *tenacity*. 'Yahweh is my shepherd.' He means Yahweh and no one else is his shepherd. He begins the psalm with *a confession of faith* and a bit of dogma. He begins by taking a stand. We must recall that Ancient Near Eastern deities were prayed to and revered under shepherding imagery: 'The shepherd Shamash [sun god] guide the people,' or 'Marduk has provided me with pasture' (see D. I. Block, *The Gods of the Nations*, 56-7). But David will have none of it. In the first line, he plants his feet, sticks his chin out, and denies pluralism—Yahweh alone is his shepherd.

And then there is a note of *sufficiency*: 'I will never lack anything.' (The 'never' is not too strong; the negative with an 'imperfect' verb can carry that sense.) This is an inference from his confession of faith. But there is no 'therefore' or 'and so' in front of it. The two statements of verse 1 are simply put side by side and we are meant to figure out the logical relation between them. Psalm 23:1 is a kind of Old Testament Romans 8:32.

With this orientation, we may press on. As Alec Motyer points out (*New Bible Commentary*), there are really three images in the psalm: sheep and Shepherd (vv. 1-3), traveler and Companion (v. 4), and guest and Host (vv. 5-6). All of these can be easily connected to the roles of the Lord Jesus Christ in the New Testament revelation. Certainly we know from John 10, for example, that the Shepherd has come in the flesh ('I am the good shepherd...and I lay down my life for the sheep'). Hence, I think it is proper to look at the geography of Psalm 23 in the light of Christ; I do not think we distort the psalm in this way but open it up.

Our first stop is at **the place of Christ's daily competence** (vv. 2-3). The stress in these verses is not so much on eating in the grassy pastures or on drinking the 'waters of rest' but on stretching out in the grass when satisfied, on the peaceful surroundings of the quiet waters, and so on the renewing of vitality ('he restores my life'). The shepherd leads in paths which he knows are the right ones. He does all this 'on account of his name,' that is, because he has a reputation he must maintain; he must show he is all that a shepherd should be, that he knows how to refresh his flock and knows where to lead his sheep. As some have pointed out, a hot, dry summer in Israel could test a shepherd's mettle, for finding pasture and water at such a time was no small trick. Or winter could be a challenge. W. M. Thomson, the nineteenth-century missionary/traveler, says that when snow covered the ground during a Lebanon winter, the shepherds could be all day up in the trees, cutting down branches, so that the sheep could feed on the green leaves and tender twigs (*The Land and the Book*, 1:303). How he supplies the day-to-day needs of the sheep says a lot about the shepherd.

All this is, we might say, the usual stuff a shepherd is to do, what we might call the bread-and-butter sort of shepherd work: he provides for his flock's ordinary and ongoing needs. Isn't this where we as Christ's sheep spend most of our time? True, many of us face severe troubles, but much of the Christian life is not lived with soap-opera tension but in the realm of the ordinary and routine. And we simply get tired. We may not get run over, we simply become run down. We suffer from wear and tear, from spiritual exhaustion. We may not get *zapped*, we just get *sapped*. Jesus Christ is the shepherd who is adequate for every day, who, again and again, 'restores my life.' And the Christian must learn to walk with Christ here in the daily round. Have you learned to enjoy Christ's day-to-day competence?

Very early in our marriage, my wife and I would do dishes together after our evening meal. She washed, I dried. In the drawer by the sink there were a number of dish towels I could use for my task. However, there was one in the stack I was not allowed to use. It had a background of white terry cloth with brightly colored vertical stripes. That dish towel was a matching 'mate' to an apron Barbara had received as part of our wedding gifts. She was afraid that if we used that towel regularly and routinely washed it, the stripes would become faded and it would no longer match the apron (which, I believe, she did not use either). It was a lovely towel, really my favorite of the whole bunch. But it was absolutely no earthly good because it could not be used on an every day basis.

Our Shepherd is not like that. It is precisely in the commonplace and familiar scenes of life where we see our

Savior's constant provision. We love Him because He does not just meet us in the critical times but in the common times. We know He will be at work for us on Tuesday and on the day after that, though there may be nothing dramatic about them. Psalm 68:19 captures it so nicely when it calls him 'the Lord, who *daily* bears us up.'

Secondly, we come to **the place of Christ's clearer presence** (v. 4). This is 'the valley of the shadow of death.' There is some debate over the word translated 'shadow of death'; some prefer something like 'deep darkness.' But the figure is reasonably clear. The ravines of Israel cut by wadis at the bottom could be treacherous to descend and arduous to climb and could harbor wild animals. All in all, a sheep's worst nightmare. So this valley signals the life-threatening, fear-generating situations of the Lord's flock. And yet we must remember, as Derek Kidner reminds us, that the valley of the shadow of death is also one of 'the paths of righteousness' (v. 3).

For all the frightfulness of the place, the psalmist has no fear of disaster. This is not because there are floodlights in the valley but because 'you are with me.' You notice here how the psalmist is snubbing you? No need to feel insulted. But notice how in verses 1-3 he has referred to Yahweh in the third person (he...he...he...); but here in verse 4 he uses the second person (you). Verses 1-3 are spoken to you, the listener/reader, *about* the Shepherd, but in verse 4 he has turned away from you and speaks *to* the Shepherd. This more intimate note occurs not in the rest and refreshment of verses 2-3 but in the darkness and distress of verse 4. It is as though the trouble in the valley drives him closer to the Shepherd and brings a deeper intimacy with Him.

Have we not often found this to be so? It is not that Christ is closer in the valley but that we realize in the valley how close He has always been.

Before we leave this stop in 'shepherd geography,' we should observe that Christ's clearer presence is also a *strong* presence. 'Your club and your staff—they comfort me.' In part, the club and staff comfort because they are tokens of the shepherd's presence—much as a hammer, saw, and tape measure imply a carpenter is near. But the shepherd also uses the club and staff; the staff to guide or control the flock, the club to beat the daylights out of the sheep's enemies. We may need a corrective here; we need to remember that a shepherd's work was hard and dangerous (see Gen. 31:38-42), and shepherds had to be 'tough hombres.' In his encyclopedic *Treasury of David,* C. H. Spurgeon includes a quotation from J. M. Porter, who described some nineteenth-century shepherds he observed, apparently in northern Transjordan:

> The shepherds themselves had none of that peaceful and placid aspect which is generally associated with pastoral life and habits. They looked like warriors marching to the battlefield—a long gun slung from the shoulder, a dagger and heavy pistols in the belt, a light battle-axe or ironheaded club in the hand. Such were the equipments; and their fierce flashing eyes and scowling countenances showed but too plainly that they were prepared to use their weapons at any moment (*Treasury of David,* 1:406).

Let this percolate in your gray matter. Let us realize that Jesus Christ, our Shepherd, is no emaciated weakling. Our Shepherd is a warrior, as shepherds had to be. No one can snatch His sheep out of His hand (John 10:28). The muscles of Jesus' arm are flexed to defend His flock; He doesn't carry a club for nothing. He is obviously enough for whatever the valley throws at us.

Our third stop comes at **the place of Christ's unstoppable provision** (v. 5)

You have likely noticed that it doesn't take much to disturb your peace while eating. That's why—at least in my adult years—I don't care for picnics, for at picnics there are either bees or flies or ants or mosquitoes or wind, or all of the above, and one simply can't relax. But if there are enemies, as here in verse 5, it's much worse. How could one even catch a snack in such circumstances? That's the odd thing about verse 5—it doesn't depict a fast gulp on the run but says, 'You prepare a table before me, right in front of my enemies.' Here is a repast that is leisurely (implied in 'you prepare a table'), festive ('you have anointed my head with fragrant oil'), and satisfying ('my cup simply runs over').

It may be fruitless to guess at the background of verse 5. But Alec Motyer (*New Bible Commentary*) makes the fascinating suggestion that just possibly David had in mind the incident of 2 Samuel 17:27-29. There David was fleeing from Absalom who had momentarily seized the throne. David arrived at Mahanaim, east of the Jordan, and there he found Shobi, Machir, and Barzillai laying in a raft of provisions for David and his loyalists. How easily David could have reflected: 'You prepare a table before me, right in front of my enemies.'

In any case, the picture in the text is clear. Danger is near and threatening, and, in the face of it, the Lord unhurriedly sustains His servant. David says, My enemies are forced to witness my enjoyment without being able to disturb it (J. A. Alexander). But sometimes the Lord's 'tables' may assume quite a literal if strange form.

Spurgeon told a story of a godly minister hurrying to escape his persecutors. He ran into a hayloft and hid himself in the hay. The soldiers came, pricking and thrusting in the hay with their swords and bayonets. One nicked the minister in the sole of his foot and left its mark. But he was undiscovered. After this, a hen came and laid an egg every day right by the place where he was hidden, and so, Spurgeon said, 'he was sustained as well as preserved until it was safe for him to leave his hiding-place.' We might prefer a 'table' with more palatable cuisine than raw eggs, but saints hiding in haylofts can't be too choosy.

However, the general principle in this text provides more assurance than particular examples. For as you look at that picture in verse 5, you must ask yourself a question: If Christ can sustain and uphold me even in the presence of my enemies, then *is there any circumstance in which Christ cannot or will not sustain His disciple?* Verse 5 should especially come home to you as you take up the bread at the Lord's Supper. (A word to the perverse: 'right in front of my enemies' does not—or should not—refer to those with you in the church fellowship!) For is that bread not a sign and a promise to you? As it comes to you, it is as if Jesus is saying to you, 'As this bread sustains your physical body, so I, your crucified and risen Lord, will never stop sustaining you—no matter what the circumstances are.'

The last locale of 'shepherd geography' is **the place of Christ's abiding rest**: 'Only goodness and faithful love will pursue me all the days of my life, and I shall turn in to the house of Yahweh for length of days' (v. 6). Let us look at the picture (6a) and the perspective (6b) in this verse.

The first part of the verse is a delightful picture. The Hebrew particle at the beginning of verse 6 can either affirm ('Surely') or restrict ('Only'). I prefer the latter, but it can go either way. But the usual translation 'follow' is too tame for the verb—it should be 'pursue.' It is a common Hebrew verb frequently used of pursuing enemies, whether, for example, Pharaoh pursuing Israel (Exod. 14:8, 9), or Israel pursuing Midianites (Judg. 7:23, 25). Here David puts a playful spin on the verb. He says that what will 'pursue' him will be Yahweh's 'goodness' (Heb., ṭôv) and 'faithful love' (ḥesed). David says it's as if Yahweh has His two special agents He sends out, ṭôv and ḥesed, and these agents are in pursuit of David, seeking to overtake him, waylay him, and dog his tracks 'all the days of his life.' But who needs to fear such beloved denizens?

Now verse 6a is not only a picture but a conviction of faith: 'Only goodness and faithful love will pursue me all the days of my life.' Is this not incredibly naïve? Not in the context of the psalm. The David who says 6a has just written verses 4-5. He has taken full stock of the valley of the shadow of death (v. 4) and of the presence of enemies (v. 5); he is not ignoring or whitewashing anything. And yet he still says, 'Only goodness and faithful love....' There is a certain chemistry in believing experience that can combine brute facts with buoyant faith. Perhaps illustration will help.

In the summer of 1680, Alan Cameron, the Covenanter, was in prison in Edinburgh and did not know that his son Richard had been killed in battle at Airds Moss[1]. A trooper

---

1   originally spelled 'Ayrsmoss'

opened the door and flung down a bloodied head and two hands, and yelled, 'Do you know whose these are?' Cameron took the gory tokens upon his knees and held them. 'Yes,' he said, 'they are my son's, my dear son's.' And then he went on: 'Good is the Lord, who could never wrong me or mine, and has made goodness and mercy to follow me all the days of my life.' It may stretch our minds, but valleys (v. 4) and enemies (v. 5) and apparently body parts do not negate the truth of verse 6a.

Now there is also a perspective we need to catch in verse 6b. Verse 6a has to do with 'all the days of my life.' Then in 6b we read, 'And I shall turn in to the house of Yahweh for length of days.' That last phrase has been traditionally translated 'forever,' but it is, literally, 'for length of days.' Some interpreters take it as synonymous with 'all the days of my life' in 6a. But that is the question: Is it? Sometimes an additional line of Hebrew poetry may say essentially the same thing as the previous line; but frequently the next line can *add to* and *say more* than what has just been said (cf. our comments on Psalm 16). The phrase 'length of days' occurs eight other times (besides here) in the Old Testament. Sometimes it may be difficult to discern whether it refers to a long present life or to ongoing life even beyond death (e.g., Ps. 91:16); but at least three times the phrase seems to pack the sense of 'forever' or 'everlastingly' (Pss. 21:4; 93:5; Lam. 5:20). This is the sense, I think, in Psalm 23:6b—David has 'upped' matters a notch. 'Length of days' speaks of something beyond 'all the days of my life.' 'Forever' is not a wrong translation here. The New Jerusalem Bible's 'for all time to come' captures the sense nicely. Now the destination has been reached. In 'the house of Yahweh' he has arrived at home. Christ's shepherding takes us safely into eternity.

Now one can look back over the journey. The grassy pastures may be the normal place, the valley of the shadows the fearful place, in front of the enemies the dangerous place, and the house of Yahweh the abiding place. And Christ leads us in—and to—them all. And so now you must go back to the beginning. What position have you taken? Only if Yahweh-Jesus is your Shepherd can you say, 'I will never lack anything—in ordinary times, in fearful times, in dangerous times, or at the last time.'

Psalm 24

Of David. A psalm.

(1) The earth and what fills it belong to Yahweh
  —the world and those who dwell in it.

(2) For **he** has laid its foundations upon the seas,
  and he establishes it upon the waters.

(3) Who can go up to the hill of Yahweh?
  And who can remain standing in his holy place?

(4) (The one with) clean hands and a pure heart,
  who has not lifted up his soul to worthlessness
    and has not gone on oath deceitfully.

(5) He will receive blessing from Yahweh,
    even vindication from the God of his salvation.

(6) This is the generation who seeks him,
  the seekers of your face, Jacob. Selah.

(7) Lift up your heads, O gates,
  and be lifted up, everlasting doors,
  and let the King of glory come in!

(8) Who is this King of glory?
  Yahweh—strong and mighty!
  Yahweh—mighty in battle!

(9) Lift up your heads, O gates,
yes, lift them up, everlasting doors,
and let the King of glory come in!

(10) Who is he, this King of glory?
Yahweh of hosts
   —he is the King of glory! Selah.

12

Ready for the King

The previous owners of our present home had a storm cellar built when they made an addition to the house. It is at a far corner of the house and is under a part of my study. One goes down to it via a short, spiral stairway and finds a room about eight by fourteen feet with shiny black tile on the floor, concrete-block walls painted white, and two lights. Imagine several archeologists about A.D. 3000, who for some reason suspect there are some old twenty-first-century buildings in this area and decide to excavate. They lay bare our storm cellar. What would they surmise? They might say it must have been a place where the family stored vegetables during the cooler months, or they might propose it was a child's bedroom. One of them might say it must have been a sort of cultic shrine—after all, the spiral stairs, the shiny black tile on the floor, the fact that there were no windows; it all points to this being a religious or devotional space. Another might posit it was a storage room for a school, especially if some of the books from my library had fallen down into it—the biblical and theological tomes along with several Agatha Christie mysteries might lead them to such a hypothesis. But all their guesses would be wrong.

It's a bit like that when scholars 'guesstimate' the life-setting of a psalm. Like Psalm 24. One may say it's part of 'the liturgy for the autumn festival,' another that it reflects David's bringing the ark of the covenant to Jerusalem in 2 Samuel 6, still another that it has in view those times when the ark arrived back at the city gate or temple entrance after it had been brought back from war. The dramatic flair of question and answer (v. 3 plus vv. 4-6, and the interchange in vv. 7-10) tempt one to posit some dramatic and lively setting. But all the guesses may be wrong. One might even wonder if the psalmist simply wrote the whole piece at one time, supplying all the graphic touches out of his own fertile memory. But that sounds so terribly unscholarly!

The primary burden of the psalm, however, is to tell Israel (and us) to be ready for the King. And if we are to be ready for the King we must realize what sort of King He is; we must realize how 'big' He is (vv. 1-2), how holy He is (vv. 3-6), and how mighty He is (vv. 7-10). Each of these sections constitutes a scenario about 'the King of glory'; hence, we will look at each in turn to get at the teaching.

First of all, we find that we have walked into **the Lord's world** in verses 1-2. The psalmist uses a little sledgehammering to make his point: his opening words are, literally, 'to Yahweh.' It is his way of 'bold-printing.' The earth and what fills it belong to Yahweh and to no one else. Both the 'stuff' ('what fills it') in the earth and the people in the world ('those who dwell in it') are Yahweh's.

I recall Dr. Walter Kaiser occasionally quoting Psalm 24:1 in class with his own twist; he might change the last of the verse to 'the world and the Assyrians that dwell in it.' He would substitute whatever might be the most frightening entity for Israel or for us in order to stress that even, for example, butchering Assyrians were subject to Yahweh's sway. Right now we might say, 'the world and the terrorists that dwell in it.' In verse 1, David simply wants to keep you from 'punifying' Yahweh, from thinking that He is simply the divine mascot of some Middle Eastern Israelite ghetto. No, the earth, the world, the whole shooting match, is His.

Why is this? Verse 2 gives the reason: 'For **he** has laid its [i.e., the earth's or the world's] foundations upon the seas, and he establishes it upon the waters.' Since Yahweh created and cares for the world (v. 2), He therefore holds possession of and sovereignty over the world (v. 1). The first pronoun in verse 2 is emphatic: He Himself and no other laid earth's foundations. The two verbs seem to refer to distinct aspects of Yahweh's world-work. The first verb definitely refers to Yahweh's past work of creation ('has laid its foundations'). The second verb is a different form of Hebrew verb that can refer to what one repeatedly does. I think that is the case here, so I have translated it as an English present tense: 'he establishes it.' Alec Motyer translates it as 'continues to maintain.' That's good. Yahweh has created and then He continues to care for and sustain what He has created. We Westerners may puzzle over the imagery, for we likely think that the seas are a rather squishy foundation and establishing something on the waters seems a pretty flimsy sort of maintenance. But the stress in the text comes from the verbs; that Yahweh 'has laid its foundations' and 'establishes' underscores that the world has a certain *stability*. So Derek Kidner says that verses 1-2 set before us a fruitful earth ('what fills it,' 1a); a peopled earth ('those who dwell in it', 1b); and a solid, or stable, earth (the verbs of v. 2).

All this matters. That Yahweh exercises worldwide sovereignty and has imposed upon and maintains an order upon his creation goes a long way toward allowing us to live in His world without ultimate fear. Let's take some time to work this out.

Most of us do not care to live or work where chaos and disorder rule. Granted, there are a few folks who seem to thrive on such bedlam but then they are strange in other ways as well. In the early days of the War between the States in my country, Simon Cameron was serving as Secretary of War for the Union cause. But by the end of 1861, President Lincoln knew he had appointed the wrong man. The position required organization and oversight in order to see that nearly 700,000 men received the supplies, training, and transport needed. Precise record-keeping was essential to keep track of contracts involving millions of dollars for rifles, cannons, horses, uniforms, blankets, and what not. Cameron's filing system consisted of scribbled notes. One congressman said that when one asked Cameron about the progress of a certain matter, he would look around for a scrap of paper, 'borrow your pencil, make a note, put the paper in one pocket of his trousers and your pencil in the other' (D. K. Goodwin, *Team of Rivals*, 403). All was mayhem.

Now that is essentially how it was in Ancient Near Eastern paganism. The Jewish scholar Nahum Sarna has written that scholars have said that Mesopotamian society suffered from 'overtones of anxiety.' The problem was theological. The nature of the pagan gods made it impossible to live in peace. In pagan belief, even deities were opposed or could be opposed to one another, and they were not above sabotaging the designs of other deities. In part of *The Epic of Gilgamesh*, Enlil and other gods decree to destroy mankind with a flood, but Ea in his own way 'leaked' the plan to Utnapishtim, warning the latter to build a ship and save his life. Then, after the gods unleashed the flood, they themselves shrank in terror and cowered like a bunch of dogs before the fury of their own wrath. Pagan deities, however, had no ultimate power. There was a realm around and beyond the gods—magic; and the gods themselves made use of magic in order to put the hex on their opponents. If that was your world, how could you have peace or sanity in it? It was like Simon Cameron's war office—everything written on snips of paper that get lost. No one is in control. One deity frustrates the design of another. It's a recipe for perpetual angst. Chaos in the highest and for that reason chaos in the heart.

But the picture in verses 1-2 of our psalm is quite different. The earth and the world belong to Yahweh alone (v. 1) and He has infused His world with a certain stability. Does this bring to mind certain New Testament texts? Like Colossians 1:17? 'And he himself [Christ] is before all things [therefore, unlike pagan deities, not a part of the world-goop] and in him all things hold together.' Or Hebrews 1:3, which assures us that Christ is continually 'upholding all things by the word of his power.' The Son of God supplies all the glue that holds the universe together.

So God has given a built-in order and cohesion to the world. Yet we must indicate, at least in general, what this means and doesn't mean. It *doesn't* mean that there will be no tornadoes or earthquakes or floods. Nor does it mean there will be no revolutions or coups. But it does mean that the promise of Genesis 8:21-22 will prove true. And because of that 'order' there is a general *predictability* in the created world, which makes both science and sanity possible. It means there is a certain *steadiness* about life in God's creation on which I can depend. So I am saved from 'overtones of anxiety' because I am not subject to flaky Ishtar but faithful Yahweh. Because the universe is held in a nail-scarred hand, I am kept from going crazy. And that seems to call for worship.

Secondly, the psalmist leads us to **the Lord's hill** in verses 3-6. 'Who can go up to the hill of Yahweh?' (v. 3a), David asks, and so he immediately sets a *marvel* before us. You sense the marvel in the assumption David makes— that one can actually approach the God of verses 1-2. He holds the world in His hands (vv. 1-2) and yet His people can meet with Him (v. 3)! Charles Spurgeon preached a sermon in 1868 on Luke 15:1, 'Then drew near unto him all the publicans and sinners for to hear him' (AV). He entitled it, 'The Approachableness of Jesus.' What a delightful way to put it. And that is the implied message here in verse 3 in its context: This God is both awesome (vv. 1-2) and approachable (v. 3)! He is both a cosmic God (vv. 1-2) and a *congregational* God (vv. 3-6); you yourself are a creature (vv. 1-2) but may also be a *communicant* (v. 3). Just the possibility, merely the suggestion, is staggering.

There may also be another marvel or surprise here, with its own twist. If we assume the Davidic origin of the psalm (see the heading), then we might ask where the 'hill of Yahweh' is. It would be in the 'city of David' (2 Sam. 5:7), where David had the ark of the covenant installed (2 Sam. 6:17). Surely not! Surely the God who created and cares for the whole vast order of creation (vv. 1-2) would not bottle up His worship in a puny hunk of real estate, confined to a mere eleven acres of a banana-shaped hill recently wrenched from the clutches of the Jebusites? That would be humiliating. That would show an utter lack of class. As some Americans would say, 'That's so red-neck.'

Paul Boller (*Presidential Anecdotes*) tells of the time Andrew Merry, the British minister to the United States, arrived at the Executive Mansion for a prearranged appointment with President Thomas Jefferson. Jefferson, who did not abide by much ceremony, came into the appointment in dressing gown and slippers. Merry was livid, his lividity perhaps aggravated by his own pomposity. But one can understand his sense of offense: one in such an exalted office should not appear in such a 'vulgar' fashion; grandeur should have no truck with grunginess.

But the Sovereign of all the earth (vv. 1-2) is not so particular, but chooses His hill in the 'sticks' and provincial backwater of the world. Once we begin to see this 'bent' to His nature we are not quite so shocked when we read John 1:14.

The Lord's hill, however, involves more than a marvel; it presents us with a *mandate* (vv. 4-5). For the Lord's hill is also 'his *holy* place' (3b)—hence those who come there must share in that holiness. Verse 4 gives us a thumbnail sketch of such holiness: a worshiper should be one with 'clean hands and a pure heart, who has not lifted up his soul to worthlessness and has not gone on oath deceitfully.' That stipulation is not meant to frustrate worship but to facilitate proper worship. We must not assume that we can go waltzing nonchalantly and casually into the presence of the Great King.

We need to pick apart verse 4 a bit. 'Hands' refers to our deeds and actions; to have 'clean' or innocent hands points to a pattern of life free from charges of wrong or inconsistency. But the psalm is concerned with the heart as well as the hands, with our disposition as well as our deeds; we are to have 'a pure heart.' One's holiness must be all-round, inward (heart) as well as outward (hands). The text insists on this twofold and proper balance. Moreover, the potential worshiper must not 'lift up his soul to worthlessness' (4b). 'Lifting up the soul (or, life)' is a way of speaking of full-fledged commitment (Pss. 25:1; 86:4; 143:8), and the word I have translated 'worthlessness' can mean a false god or idol (see NIV; and Ps. 31:6; Jer. 18:15; Jonah 2:8). There can be no divided affections; one's devotion must be to Yahweh alone. Finally, the one coming to the Lord's hill must not have 'gone on oath deceitfully' (4c). His speech is marked by integrity. He doesn't swear false oaths in order to gain advantage of people. All this is fairly rigorous. Our deeds and dispositions and affections and words are placed under scrutiny. And if you have any sensitivity of conscience at all you may throw up your hands and despair of coming into the King's presence.

Such despair would be a wrong response, for then you would be forgetting that what the Lord requires He also gives. An earnest Israelite could have had the same 'Who-then?' reaction. And the answer to such a despairing

Israelite is in Yahweh's words in Leviticus 17:11: 'I have given it [the blood] for you on the altar to make atonement for your souls' (ESV). There is a way back to clean hands and a pure heart and right affections and truthful speech—in the atoning blood of sacrifice that covers it all. The Christian's recourse is essentially the same: we are driven back to 'the blood of Jesus his Son that keeps on cleansing us from every sin' (1 John 1:7).

So I must not allow verse 4 to turn me away from the Lord's hill and holy place. If it brings me to conviction, I must let conviction have its perfect work and lead me to repentance and restoration. Nothing bad about that. In Iain Murray's one-volume biography of Martyn Lloyd-Jones, he speaks of varied responses to Dr. Lloyd-Jones' preaching in his days at Westminster Chapel. One of the regulars at the Chapel in the 1950s was Emmi Müller, a German girl studying at London Bible College. Ms. Müller said, 'Time and again coming home from church I went straight to my room, locked my door, and went on my knees and prayed.' Was that bad, that preaching did that to her? Certainly not. And if the mandate in verse 4 disturbs us, that is not bad—if it leads us to repentance and restores us to the Lord's holy place, where His worshipers are accepted, receiving blessing and ultimate vindication from their saving God (v. 5).

Perhaps the most puzzling but fascinating matter, however, in verses 3-6 is the *model* set before us. This appears in verse 6. The first of verse 6 seems to sum up verses 3-5, as if to say, Now these (especially the folks of vv. 4-5) are the sort of people who seek Yahweh. And then the last of verse 6 turns strange: 'the seekers of your face, Jacob.' The 'seekers of your [Yahweh's] face' is simply a reference back to 6a, referring to genuine worshipers of Yahweh. But what is this 'Jacob' doing here? That's all there is in the text—simply the name Jacob.

Some of the ancient versions have 'the God of Jacob' here and some of our English translations have adopted that (e.g., NIV, ESV). But one suspects the ancient versions were simply doing their best to make sense out of a tough text. One proposal that is a bit more anchored to the Hebrew text is to translate 'like Jacob.' At least that seems to point in the right direction. 'Jacob' is parallel to 'the generation' (6a) that seeks Yahweh and seems to be laid down as a sample of the 'seekers of your face.' When might this have been? One thinks of that episode in Genesis 32 when Jacob said, 'I have seen God face to face, and yet my life has been delivered' (v. 30). What might have been so exemplary about Jacob on that occasion? Was it not his *attitude*, that even at the risk of his life he insisted, 'I will not let you go unless you bless me' (v. 26)?

Proposing Jacob as a model for anything makes some people nervous. They have read the Genesis narratives; they know all about the scheming, prevaricating, devious life Jacob led. But, of course, no one—least of all Psalm 24— is proposing Jacob as a model across the board. During my country's Civil War, a number of President Lincoln's own party were disturbed over reports of General U.S. Grant's alleged drunkenness and fondness for the bottle. One of their spokesmen once pressed the matter on Lincoln far into the night. After all had been said, Lincoln remained silent for the longest time. At last he gathered himself up and said: 'I can't spare this man—he fights!' Lincoln was not approving Grant's alleged affection for whiskey; he was not making a judgment on whether Grant was responsible for the various 13,000 Union casualties at the Battle of Shiloh, or whether he liked or disliked the lack of spit and polish in Grant's military dress. Rather, there was simply one thing: he fights. He does, Lincoln would have said, what I cannot get my other generals to do; here at least is one commander who seems to know that war is for fighting!

I suggest that is the way Jacob is held up here in verse 6: as a model in only one matter. He knew how to hold on to God for dear life. 'I will not let you go unless you bless me.' In that sense, there need to be more Jacob clones in Yahweh's holy place, ones with the Jacob-attitude that refuses to let go of God until He blesses them. This implies, at least in part, that many of the worshipers at the Lord's hill are *desperate* people holding on to Yahweh by their fingernails because they know they have nowhere else to turn.

The third section of the psalm, verses 7-10, pictures **the Lord's coming**. As I noted at the very beginning of this exposition, it is very difficult to be certain of the original setting of this psalm, or even parts of it. If, in spite of my skepticism, I had to choose a setting for verses 7-10, I would likely settle for the view that sees the ark of the covenant arriving at the gates of the city of David after Israel's troops had enjoyed victory on the field of battle. The ark signified Yahweh's presence, and when it arrived it was as if he arrived. And the catechetical question-and-answer simply ratchets up the drama of the ark's—and Yahweh's—return. Additionally, there is some evidence that verses 7-10 contain a dig at Canaanite paganism, but we cannot take time to flesh that out.

Let us go to the heart of these verses. If the 'King of glory' has come, what is He like? Or, as the text itself asks, 'Who is this King of glory?' On the one hand verse 8 answers, 'Yahweh—strong and mighty! Yahweh—mighty in battle!' And verse 10 answers, 'Yahweh of hosts,' Yahweh who has all resources at His disposal. Why is such a king so glorious and thrilling for the people of God?

Let us for a moment join Christiana and her children in the latter part of Bunyan's *The Pilgrim's Progress*. Mr. Great-heart is serving as their guide to the Celestial City and at one point they come upon a man 'with his sword drawn and his face all bloody.' He identified himself as Valiant-for-truth. He was bloody because he had just come through a three-hour combat against Wild-head, Inconsiderate, and Pragmatic, who were determined to liquidate him. They wounded him, he wounded them, and they had taken to their heels. It's at this point that Great-heart asks to see Valiant-for-Truth's sword and, when he examines it, calls it, in that nifty Bunyanism, 'a right Jerusalem blade.' But the scene is Bunyan's way of saying, once more, that Christian pilgrimage is a war, a battle; the Christian life is combat and conflict. Christ's servants get bloodied up and beaten up. It's a time when 'fierce temptation' seems to 'threaten hard to bear us down' (John Newton).

Now if all this is the case, does it not mean that the King of glory is truly glorious precisely because He is 'Yahweh—strong and mighty! Yahweh—mighty in battle!'? How heartening to know that through all the years Yahweh has never ceased to be a warrior (Exod. 15:3). The glorious

King is, of course, glorious in all our circumstances, be they afflictions, conflicts, or routines. But His being 'mighty in battle' shows how His nature is adapted to our needs, for that description tells us Yahweh is not only the God of the sanctuary but of the field, not merely the God of the shrine but of the marketplace, not only the God of the church but of the foxhole. I plead with you not to allow those who only want to speak of a 'Jesus-meek-and-mild' to rob you of the manly, virile comfort of having a God who is mighty in battle. Jesus, the King of glory, will come as a warrior at the last (Rev. 19:11-21) and, thankfully, how often He also 'comes' in the midst of our current troubles to bash to bits the fetters of the enemy and to take up the cudgels for His weary and crushed people. You have no comfort if the King of glory is a wimp who reeks of hand cream; you only have solace if he is your Defender in the thick of war.

Perhaps the best way to rub Psalm 24 into the pores of your soul would be to use it in worship—either individually or in our family circles. Take Bible and hymnbook. Read verses 1 and 2, and then sing Joachim Neander's 'Praise to the Lord, the Almighty, the King of Creation.' Then read verses 3-6 and respond with George Croly's 'Spirit of God, Descend upon My Heart.' Finally, read verses 7-10 and join in 'Come, Thou Almighty King.'

the
W a y
o f t h e
Righteous
in the
Muck
of Life

Psalms 1-12

Dale Ralph Davis

paperback ISBN 978-1-84550-581-3
epub ISBN 978-1-84550-673-5
Mobi ISBN 978-1-78191-039-9

The Way of the Righteous in the Muck of Life

Psalms 1–12

DALE RALPH DAVIS

In the opening pages of the Psalms, believers discover foundational truth for right living and great delight as children of God. Trusted theologian Dale Ralph Davis leads readers through a careful study of Psalms 1–12 with clear application for daily life.

As the first 12 Psalms continue, we see basic principles unfold with great clarity. Much like our troubles today, the Psalmist endured wickedness all around, a world hostile to the true God and on a very personal level deceit and persecution from his enemies. Readers are pointed toward the glorious rule of the Messiah, to whom the whole world belongs. In light of this realization, we are prepared to face all kinds of troubles that could cause despair. The righteous rely on God, and the Psalms teach us how. This book is ideal for use by small groups, as a teaching guide or for reference.

Dale Ralph Davis and his wife live in rural Tennessee. Prior to that, he was pastor of Woodland Presbyterian Church, Hattiesburg, Mississippi and Professor of Old Testament at Reformed Theological Seminary, Jackson, Mississippi. Davis has also written several commentaries for the Focus on the Bible series: *Joshua, Judges, 1 Samuel, 2 Samuel, 1 Kings,* and *2 Kings;* and other books such as *The House that Jesus Built* and *The Word Became Fresh.*

Christian Focus Publications

Our mission statement —

STAYING FAITHFUL

In dependence upon God we seek to impact the world through literature faithful to His infallible Word, the Bible. Our aim is to ensure that the Lord Jesus Christ is presented as the only hope to obtain forgiveness of sin, live a useful life and look forward to heaven with Him.

Our Books are published in four imprints:

CHRISTIAN FOCUS

popular works including biographies, commentaries, basic doctrine and Christian living.

CHRISTIAN HERITAGE

books representing some of the best material from the rich heritage of the church.

MENTOR

books written at a level suitable for Bible College and seminary students, pastors, and other serious readers. The imprint includes commentaries, doctrinal studies, examination of current issues and church history.

CF4•K

children's books for quality Bible teaching and for all age groups: Sunday school curriculum, puzzle and activity books; personal and family devotional titles, biographies and inspirational stories—because you are never too young to know Jesus!

Christian Focus Publications Ltd,
Geanies House, Fearn, Ross-shire,
IV20 1TW, Scotland, United Kingdom.
www.christianfocus.com
blog.christianfocus.com